# Throwing & Handbuilding

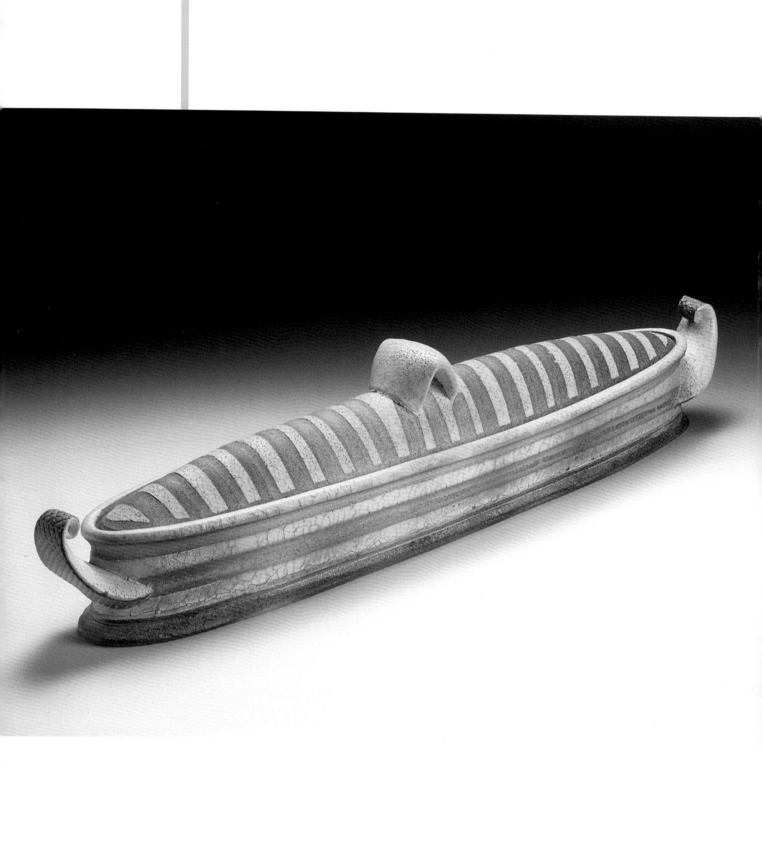

Forming
Techniques

# Throwing
# & Handbuilding

Ceramic
Arts
Handbook
Series

*Edited by Anderson Turner*

The American Ceramic Society
735 Ceramic Place, Suite 100
Westerville, Ohio 43081

www.CeramicArtsDaily.org

The American Ceramic Society
735 Ceramic Place, Suite 100
Westerville, OH 43081

11  10  09  08  07    5  4  3  2  1

ISBN: 978-1-57498-289-3

Publisher: Charles Spahr, President, Ceramic Publications Company, a wholly owned subsidiary of The American Ceramic Society

Art Book Program Manager: Bill Jones

Series Editor: Anderson Turner

Graphic Design and Production: Melissa Bury, Bury Design, Westerville, Ohio

Cover: Teapot by Scott Dooley, vase by Gabriel Brubacher, and slab plate by Jan Schachter.

Frontispiece: Covered serving dish by Bruce Cochrane

Photo credits: All photos by authors or artists except for the following: John Escosa (25-27); Harrison Evans (29); Donna Crietzberg (30-34); Bohemian Nomad and John Cornicello (52-58); Don Anderson (94-96); Eva Heyd and Bruce Ostwald (119-126); Michael Harvey (127-130); Hap Sakwa (131-134).

Printed in China

# Contents

# Preface

I love the initial rush of beginning to make a new work of art out of clay. Whatever the piece is, the first moments of deciding what clay to use and how much,
have continuously been hopeful and fun moments throughout my life. Further,
I get a lot out of the immediacy of this material. Very few other materials offer a complete tactile experience like clay does and that sense that "now we're
making something".

However, there is more to making a piece out of clay than grabbing a hunk
and sitting down at a table or wheel. Sketching out ideas on paper or even
making a small 3-D model out of clay are approaches people often take before
starting out. Further, there are several technical issues of how to make the desired piece that one needs to consider. Perhaps the best thing to help you learn
how to make a functional or non-functional piece is to make it several times.
Move a lot a material and you have the opportunity to figure out the technical
issues along the way. Also, many if not most of the issues one might have with
the form itself can be overcome by just making more.

This book is filled with people who have been inspired by the artistic and
technical challenges that clay brings. Each artist has chosen to share a unique
idea or fresh approach resulting from years of practice and thought. Still, there
remains a level of spontaneity, too, that is unique to this medium as well as a
sense of joy in the material. These thoughts and ideas are a great resource for
inspiration and a boon to anyone's technical handbook.

*Anderson Turner*

# Throwing Large Plates and Platters

*by Samuel L. Hoffman*

Ceramic plates and platters are some of the most functionally useful forms you can make. They also provide wonderful surfaces for artistic expression and creativity. However, the process of creating a plate or platter does not merely entail squashing a piece of clay into a flat disc. In fact, when subjected to the high temperatures of glaze firing, a poorly crafted platter will inevitably crack, warp, or deform in some manner. Here are several different techniques for throwing and trimming that help eliminate some of the problems inherent to making large plates and platters.

(Top) Stoneware plate, 12 inches in diameter, reduction fired in a gas kiln, carbon-trap shino glaze with wax resist brushwork.

(Bottom) Porcelain platter, 24 inches in diameter, wood fired in the Kent State University (Ohio) anagama, natural ash glaze and atmospheric flashing.

## Throwing a Platter from a Single Ball of Clay

It's relatively easy to throw a large plate (up to 15 inches) from a single ball of clay. When making plates, it's advisable to use clay that is slightly wetter than when throwing vertically oriented pieces. First, wedge a large bit of clay (6-8 lbs.), taking care to eliminate any air pockets that may be present.

Pound the clay into a ball and slap it down onto a clean, dry bat that is mounted on the wheel head (figure 1). Wet the clay and begin centering with both hands opposite each other, compressing the clay into the shape of a cone. When the cone of clay is basically on center, begin pressing down on the top with the fingers or palm of one hand, while keeping the sides centered with the other hand (figure 3). Make sure to keep the clay surface well lubricated with water, as dry spots can produce asymmetries or irregularities that will be emphasized during firing. Keep compressing the clay until it nears the edge of the bat (figure 4).

When you have established the approximate diameter of the plate, use a sponge to compress the clay from the center to the edge, going back and forth several times, smoothing out the surface (figure 5). Some potters like to further compress and

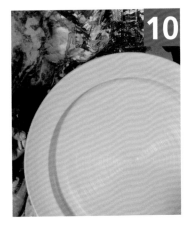

flatten the plate with the use of a wooden or rubber rib (figure 6).

Now that the general shape of the plate is established, it is time to finish the rim. Compress the rim while raising it slightly above the surface of the plate (figure 7). Carefully throw the rim into the desired shape, taking care not to make it too thin to support its own weight. Remember, excess clay can always be removed in the trimming stage (figure 8).

Using a sponge, clean up the plate and remove any slurry that has built up. Take a wooden knife and carefully cut a 45° angle into the foot of the plate to allow for easier cut-off and trimming (figure 9). Unless you use plaster bats for throwing, which do not require cut-off, pulling a wire tool under a large plate can be one of the trickiest parts of the process. A cut-off wire naturally raises up in the middle of a plate, creating a thin spot that can develop a warp or crack. Rather than cutting the piece off by pulling a wire under the base in a single motion, break it up into two steps. First, use a wire tool lon-

ger than the diameter of the plate. Then, before moving the wire to the far side of the plate, pull the wire several inches under the front side of the plate (nearest your lap) while the wheel is spinning (figure 10). This should free the outside edge of the plate from the bat. Remove the wire, then move it to the far side of the plate and pull it all the way under the plate as the wheel spins. By initially cutting several inches under the plate, there is less drag when you pull the wire completely through (figure 11), preventing the wire from raising up and cutting off too much from the middle of the plate.

## Throwing a Platter from Several Balls of Clay

As the size of a platter increases, it becomes more difficult to center the large amount of clay from a single ball. Instead of using one 15 lb. ball of clay, wedge up two or three 4-6 lb. pieces. Place the first ball on a bat in the same manner as described above, but do not wet the clay (figure 1). While the wheel is slowly turning, use a slapping motion with both hands on opposite sides of the clay to center the ball without flattening it out too much. Next, slam the second ball of clay down on the first and re-center the mound using the same rhythmic slapping (figure 2).

When this process is repeated with the third ball (figure 3), it becomes evident that quite a large amount of clay can be centered with minimal physical exertion. After all of the clay has been slap-centered into a cone, begin pounding the center of the clay and flattening it into a disc (figure 4). Remember, at this point the wheel is still spinning slowly and no water has been used (figure 5). Using soft clay, it is possible to pound the clay all the way out to the edge of the bat, keeping it centered with the rhythmic slapping of both hands (figure 6).

As soon as the clay is flattened and centered, use a wet sponge to smooth out the surface and compress the platter (figure 7).

When throwing a large platter, it becomes difficult to estimate the thickness of the base. It is important to leave enough clay for a well-trimmed foot ring. If necessary, insert a needle tool into the center of the platter to determine how thick the base is (figure 8).

Finish the rim in the same manner as described above, taking care to leave enough clay to support the rim's weight. Smooth and clean up the surface of the platter with a sponge (figure 9). Make a 45° bevel into the foot and cut off the platter using the same two-step process described before (figure 10).

Like any ceramic process, this throwing technique takes practice to master. However, the potential for using these large forms as ceramic canvases for artistic expression makes plates and platters some of the most exciting pieces a potter can make.

## Trimming a Large Platter

Before trimming, it is important to slowly dry the platter under plastic to avoid uneven stiffness.

While some problems inherent with making plates and platters are eliminated in the throwing stage other problems are mitigated during trimming stage. Due to the large size of platters, they undergo a significant amount of stress during the firing process. Although it is possible to make a successful platter that is not trimmed, the strongest way to finish a piece involves creating a foot ring. Trimming compresses the underside of a platter making it less susceptible to cracking. Additionally, foot rings allow you to glaze both sides of the platter, creating a very

strong glaze/clay/glaze finish. However, when dealing with platters of large scale, it becomes increasingly difficult to flip and trim the piece without distorting it.

When the clay is leather hard, and leaving the platter on the bat, place a sponge, towel, or other soft object in the center to prevent the center from slumping during trimming (figure 1). Carefully place a large bat on top of the rim of the platter (figure 2). Support the platter with one hand underneath the bottom bat and place one hand on top (figure 3).

In one smooth motion, flip the platter while sandwiching it between both hands (figure 4). Place the bottom bat onto the wheelhead and remove the top bat to expose the underside of the platter (figure 5). Use three soft balls of clay to hold the platter down on the large bat, taking care not to deform the rim (figure 6).

Using a sharp trimming tool, begin removing clay from the outside edge of the platter (figure 7). Finish trimming the outer edge of the foot, establishing the diameter of the foot ring (figure 8).

Establish the inside edge of the large foot ring, then begin trimming the small foot in the center of the platter, tapping the clay to listen for the thickness of the base. Finish the inside foot and continue removing clay until the desired thickness is achieved (figure 9). Finish trimming the outside foot and clear away loose clay (figure 10).

Smooth both foot rings with a damp sponge, taking care not to wet the clay too much (figure 11).

## Trimming Platters with Altered Rims

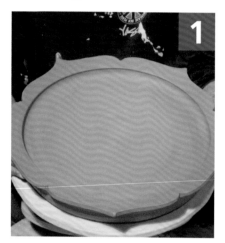

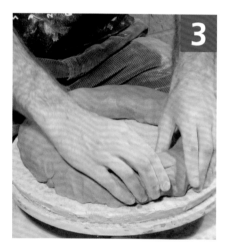

Altering the circular form of a plate is an exciting means of expression for ceramic artists, but can present difficulties at the trimming stage (figure 1).

If the rim of a plate is cut or manipulated into an asymmetrical shape, or is delicate, the piece cannot simply be inverted onto another bat for trimming (figure 2). Instead, the piece must be placed on a clay chuck that supports the plate in the center. To create this chuck, form a large coil from the same clay body

that the plate was made from.

Attach the coil to the wheel head in the shape of a donut, making sure that enough height is established to hold the plate above the wheel head (figure 3).

Flatten and smooth the coil using as little water as possible, creating a rounded cushion on which to rest the plate (figure 4). It is important to let the plate stiffen up a little bit more than usual before trimming to avoid flexing or chipping the altered lip when the piece is inverted.

Leaving the plate on the bat it was thrown on, carefully flip the plate onto the palm of one hand or a small bat the fits the center of the plate (figure 5).

Place the upside-down plate onto the coil and make sure that it is centered (figure 6). Gently press down on the middle of the plate to create a vacuum that will hold the piece in place (figure 7). Start trimming by removing excess clay from the outside of the plate.

Trim the plate using the same techniques described before, taking care to avoid the delicate lip that hangs over the wheel head (figure 8). When the foot rings are trimmed, smooth the bottom of the plate and carefully remove it from the coil. If the inside surface of the plate has been marred from resting on the coil, use a sponge to clean it up.

## Mounting a platter

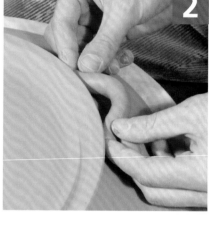

Although plates and platters are traditionally used horizontally for serving on a table, they can be prepared for hanging on the wall (figure 1). One technique is to punch holes into the outer foot ring that can later be used for hanging with wire or string. Use one hole if you want to determine the orientation of the platter. Pierce several holes to allow the owner of the piece to determine the best way to hang it.

Another method of preparing a platter for hanging is to attach a simple coil of clay as a loop at the top of the piece, taking care that it does not protrude below the foot ring when the piece is sitting flat (figure 2). This clay loop can be hung directly on a nail or can be used to attach a wire or string to the platter for mounting. It is possible to purchase prefabricated plate hangers, but most of these protrude over the edge of the piece, creating a visual distraction that takes away from the integrity of the rim.

Porcelain platter, 17 inches in diameter, reduction fired in a gas kiln, carbon-trap shino glaze with wax resist brushwork.

Porcelain platter, 22 inches in diameter, reduction fired in a gas kiln, carbon-trap shino glaze with wax resist brushwork.

# Bruce Cochrane
## Up in Canada

*by Tony Clennell*

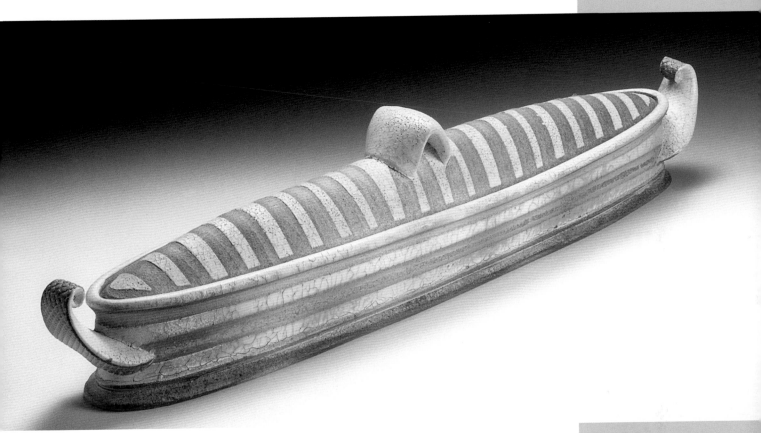

**Covered serving dish, 22 inches in length, thrown and slab-built stoneware, wood fired.**

Up in Canada, there's this guy named Bruce Cochrane. Around here, the mere mention of his given name instantly identifies Bruce and the excellence of his work.

I have watched Bruce's career unfold over the years. I have witnessed an educator building a ceramics program with a notable reputation and a potter honing his craft. A tour of our rather extensive clay collection always begins with a 24-inch-diameter Shino-glazed plate purchased at Bruce's show at Prime Gallery in Toronto some two decades ago. The plate is so strong and the decoration is so casual. It has thick, ladled slip trails and fingerwipes through the glaze. It is the piece that if our house was on fire and I had to make a choice, I'd grab it and run.

One evening, I was enjoying a bourbon with Georgia potter/educator Ron Meyers when he said that on the workshop circuit almost everyone gets around to making an oval dish. When Meyers makes one in a demo, someone invariably asks if he could demonstrate the making of a

Covered serving dish, 24 inches in length, thrown and slab-built stoneware, glazed, salt fired.

lid for the oval. His standard answer is "Up in Canada, there's this guy named Bruce. This is the guy that does it well!"

A homegrown talent, Bruce was born in Vancouver, British Columbia, and moved to Montreal, Quebec, at the age of ten. He was introduced to ceramics at John Abbott College, where he was inspired by his first instructor, Julia Manitius, to continue his education with Walter Ostrom at the Nova Scotia College of Art and Design. He attended the New York State College of Ceramics at Alfred University, where he earned an M.F.A. Returning to Canada, he took a position at Sheridan College. A little more than two decades later—thanks to Bruce's dedication to clay and his students—Sheridan is recognized as having one of Canada's best ceramics programs.

Utility continues to serve as the foundation for his ideas. "The pots I make, no matter how simple or complex, large or small, are meant to be experienced on a physical and visual level," he commented. "The way an object carries, lifts, cradles, pours and contains are the properties I strive to make engaging for the user, offering more than just convenience.

"After the thinking and drawing stages, the development of an idea occurs by working in multiples. The serial approach keeps me focused on solving problems at hand, but also presents, at various stages throughout the process, numerous tangents for other work."

"It seems that the contemporary potters whose work has impact and a strong sense of the maker are those who make connections to ce-

**Covered bowl, 17 inches in height, press-molded stoneware, with wheel-thrown elements, salt fired.**

ramics history," Bruce observed. "It is such a vast source of inspiration, it's hard to ignore. I live in a house that is filled with folk pottery from our own North American tradition, China and a lesser number of European examples.

"On my recent trip to China, the robust yet formal character of the bronze vessels in the Shanghai Museum, the simplicity and texture of rural architecture, and the energy and technology involved in the massive ceramic production in general provided a starting point for much of my new work. The use of press-molded forms combined with thrown elements has facilitated the development of these new ideas. It allows for greater scale and more extreme form, as well as practical means of fit."

Bruce's new work includes large squared bowls that could quite easily be used to bathe young children. The teapots are gallon sized and the oval trays are the size of a one-man dugout canoe. The long oval casseroles with fitted lids look like covered longboats. Most are salt-fired stoneware, with slips and glazes ap-

Three jars on a stand, 9 inches in height, thrown and press-molded porcelain jars on stoneware stand, wood fired.

Teapot, 10 inches in height, thrown and altered porcelain, glazed, salt fired.

plied over tape-masked patterns to reinforce the geometry of form. The scale, the mastery of craft, the quiet surface decoration and the attention to detail are remarkable.

Bruce has created a magical place at Sheridan with a strong aesthetic attitude toward pots. This is not a narrow aesthetic, since we have seen him work with low-fire earthenware (glazed and wood fired), as well as wood-fired and salt-glazed stoneware and porcelain.

"The idea comes first, followed by selection of material and process," Bruce explained. "If the idea doesn't fit, I change the technology. This [approach] is also a result of having to understand a wide range of methodology as a teacher at a school that offers that diversity."

A shallow, bottomless cylinder with a lid seat (gallery) is thrown on the wheel (figure 1).

The wet cylinder is cut off and positioned on an oval slab (figure 2).

The base and wall are joined inside and out, and the edge is scalloped by pushing with opposing fingers (figure 3).

Once the excess clay at the base has been removed, handles are attached to both ends (figure 4).

When leather hard, the vessel is covered with plastic and a soft slab, similar in size to the one used for the base, is placed on top to form the lid (figure 5).

The lid slab is then worked into the cavity of the vessel; in this case, the scalloped-edge design is transferred to the lid as well (figure 6).

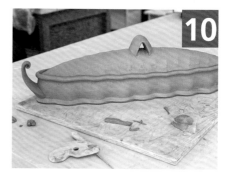

After the lid is dry enough to support its own weight, excess clay is trimmed from the edge and a handle is added (figure 7).

When the handled lid is soft leather hard, it is positioned in the lid seat (figure 8).

The edge of the lid is then manipulated to form a tight fit (figure 9).

The finished piece is dried slowly with the lid in place, to ensure a proper fit and avoid warping (figure 10).

**Covered serving dish, 20 inches in length, thrown and slab-built stoneware, salt fired, by Bruce Cochrane, Mississauga, Ontario, Canada.**

# Teapot Gems
## Dazzling Compact Forms

*by Fong Choo*

For more than a decade I've been exploring the teapot in its miniaturized form. The teapot form continues to challenge and fascinate me, and the idea of doing one thing and doing it well has been central to the success of my profession as a potter. There are a lot of techniques involved in making these teapots, and some of the techniques require tools that I have made for myself to suit a certain situation.

Although a native of Singapore, I attended college in North Carolina with graduate work in Kentucky at the University of Louisville. I'm inspired by my Chinese heritage, and particularly in the long tradition of Yixing pottery. My teapots are small and jewel-like, made of porcelain and often fired to cone 6 in an electric kiln.

**Teapot, 6 inches in height, porcelain, fired to cone 6. This teapot is glazed with what Choo calls his "Crystal Celadon" glaze, which is a layered combination of commercial glazes (Amaco Textured Alligator, LT Series and LT 122 Dark Blue)**

You can get wonderful glaze effects by spraying on an even coat of a cone 6 glaze then brushing on cone 06 glazes. Test applications before use.

**"Low Rider Teapot," 6 inches in height, porcelain, fired to cone 6. The lid for this teapot was made like the one in the demonstration. The glazed surface was created by layering the entire piece with three coats of Mayco CG 716 Pagoda Green (crystal glaze). The shoulder was then glazed with one coat of Duncan Spanish Moss 20065 (Crystaltone glaze).**

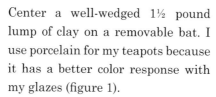

Center a well-wedged 1½ pound lump of clay on a removable bat. I use porcelain for my teapots because it has a better color response with my glazes (figure 1).

It is important not to overwork the clay, especially in the early stages of the process. In three passes, you should have the approximate form (figure 2).

I use a push stick to expand and redefine the form (figure 3). I follow the push stick on the outside with a metal rib to smooth the surface and remove excess moisture.

One feature I like to add to many of my teapots is a "moat." It provides not only a visual base for the teapot, but also functions as a glaze catch (figure 4).

Begin the moat with a rounded tool and push in and down into the base. Using a bevel tool, round over the edge and move the tool underneath to provide lift (figure 5).

Next, I alter the teapot with a rib in a couple of passes, creating an interesting movement within the shape (figure 6).

I use a small roller and further alter the gesture of the form. After completing these alterations, I wire off the piece and remove it with the bat to set up (figure 7).

To create a spout, roll out a tapered coil then push a stick into it. With the stick inside, roll the coil to expand it (figure 8). Once the spout is soft leather hard, cut it to the appropriate length, trim the end and attach it to the teapot body (figure 9).

Adjust the spout to the correct angle and add pouring holes (figure 10).

For the feet, roll and taper 3-inch coils. Gently flatten one side of the coil, then pick it up and curl each end toward the center. Set aside until soft leather hard (figure 11).

For the handle, roll out a 6-inch coil that's tapered on each end. Shape the handle into an interesting shape and set aside until soft leather hard (figure 12). I throw lids off the hump using a small homemade tool (figure 13). A finished teapot. The teapots are bisque fired then glazed with commercial cone 06–04 glazes combined with cone 6 glazes, and final fired to cone 6 in oxidation (figure 14).

# Staying Trim
## Working with Porcelain

*by Antoinette Badenhorst*

**Pedestal pot, glazed with a red glaze on the inside with water etching outside and the rim cut out. Electric fired to cone 10.**

My initial experience with porcelain came early in my pottery career. Even though I had just started feeling I was in control of my clay and glazing, I had heard and read about porcelain and was eager to take on another challenge. After managing to throw some decent casseroles, I thought nothing could stop me. Little did I know that there is much more to porcelain than the ability to throw it on a wheel. My first firing was a disaster. Some pieces stuck to the kiln shelf, all of the pieces were deformed, and colors that worked in stoneware were stark and unattractive in porcelain. It would be another seven years before I tried again, and after five years of working with it, I've developed a respect for porcelain that will last a lifetime.

Another event in my life had an important influence on my work. I was once confronted by a customer for not having foot rims on my vases. Maybe he was just looking for an excuse not to buy any of my pieces, but the incident has lasted a lifetime. Whether he was right or wrong

doesn't matter. His comment made me look critically at my work, and that was the biggest gift I have ever received from a customer.

As the years have gone by and I've developed my own style in throwing, it has become more and more essential for me to trim a foot rim on nearly every piece I throw. The need for some type of base to support the vertical movement of a piece has become a part of my own observation of my work. In working with porcelain, I have expanded the trimming process beyond foot rims to include the entire form, and I now consider trimming to be the most important part of the throwing process.

### Throwing

Before throwing porcelain, it's important to adequately plan and design what you'll be making. Porcelain contains more silica and feldspar (the glass-making components in clay bodies) and less clay (the plasticizers in clay bodies), so the body is very open and porous.

This means that it is more difficult to work with than other clays since it becomes saturated with water so quickly and collapses much faster.

For best results, wedge porcelain twice: once a little earlier—even a day—then right before use. Once you have centered the clay, coning is also important. Use removable bats to throw on.

When opening the clay, pay attention to the original planning of the bowl. Most of the bowls I create are curved in the bottom so I start with curving the inside. The first two pulls of the clay are quick and intended to create height for the basic shape (figure 1).

Use just enough water or slurry to keep a wall of clay moving above your fingers (figure 2). The slightest dryness can distort the bowl and you might have to start over, so use a sponge to control the release of moisture. Since porcelain is very thirsty and readily absorbs water, it quickly becomes too soft to work and control. Frequently clean water from the inside and make sure the original contour of the bottom is still in place (figure 3).

Thin, shape and compact the walls with the tip of your wet fingers (figure 4). Then, with the wheel at a medium speed, use as much time as needed to create the desired shape

on the inside of the bowl. If the inside shape is successful, you can easily trim the outside to follow the inside since it is easier to trim unwanted clay away from the outside.

Use two plastic kidneys, one on the inside and one outside, to squeegee excess slip off and eliminate throwing rings without distorting the form (figure 5). Leave extra clay on the bottom of the sides to provide extra support until the form sets up (figure 6).

## Trimming

About 30 minutes after you've finished throwing, cover the piece and protect it from uneven drafts. With porcelain, you don't want the rims to dry out too fast. You also want to avoid uneven drying, which causes cracking and warping in many porcelain pieces rather than the speed at which it is drying.

Once the piece has reached firm leather hard, return it to the wheel in an upright position and attach it to the plaster bat. Using very sharp tools, trim away any ridges and thick parts on the inside of the bowl. Use a round loop tool that follows the inside curve of the bowl (figure 7). A metal kidney helps create a smooth surface (figure 8). Follow with a damp sponge and a rubber kidney to compact the clay.

Trim the unwanted thickness on the outside using a sharp pointed wooden tool (figure 9). Next, with the pot still upright and on the bat, use a loop tool to trim excess clay and throwing marks from the outside surface (figure 10). Continue trimming the whole form until you get the thinness you want. It's easier to work faster and more aggressively while the clay is still fairly soft and the walls thicker. However, when the clay is soft, it's easy to cut too deep or create an uneven surface. As the walls become thinner and drier, use a lighter touch and sharper tools.

Since the bottom is still attached to the bat, you can accurately judge the wall thickness without having to handle the pot too much. Porcelain becomes dry quickly and the thin walls need very careful and limited handling to prevent them from cracking.

By the time the clay releases itself from the plaster bat, it's dry enough to trim the foot rim. Very carefully place the bowl with the rim down and centered on a foam-covered bat (figure 11). The bat has holes that fit onto the pins on the wheel head and the foam is marked with rings to help me find the center with the least handling of the pot.

Using a Surform blade (figure 12), remove any bumps and roughness

created by the cutoff tool. The final step is to create the shape you originally planned trimming with a series of contoured loop tools (figure 13). I carefully choose tools that allow me to create the right curve at the bottom, and I also trim the whole piece again right down to the rim (figure 14).

The last tool needed to finish is a metal kidney. Trim the final unevenness away and follow with a damp sponge and a plastic kidney to compact the clay.

By now the whole action becomes a fine balance between the character of the clay and the skill of the potter. If that stays in harmony, it is possible to create beautiful pottery.

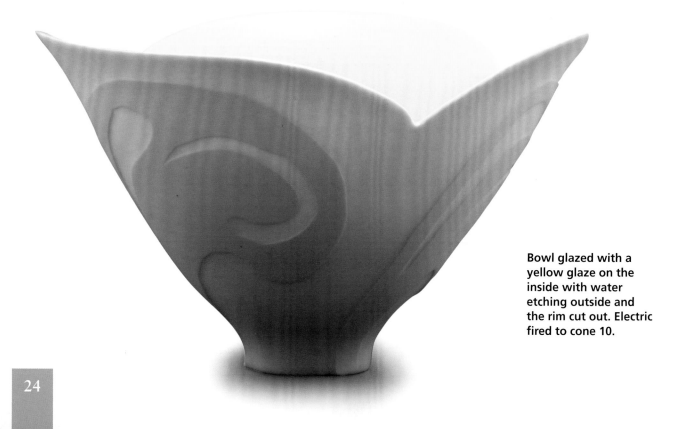

**Bowl glazed with a yellow glaze on the inside with water etching outside and the rim cut out. Electric fired to cone 10.**

# Rebecca Coffman
## Spirited Vessels

*by Nancy McCroskey*

W ork by Rebecca Coffman reveals her love of the medium and joy in the creative process. Coffman, an associate professor of art at Huntington College in Huntington, Indiana, produced these pots at the University of Delaware while on sabbatical leave.

In developing this series, Coffman used a variety of altering and additive processes. Thrown without bases, the forms were dropped, paddled, stretched and assembled throughout the wet and leather-hard stages.

Early on, after some pots had been fired, a friend poured hot water into one of the new teapots. To Coffman's dismay, it cracked. When mixed with the clays that were on hand at the University of Delaware, the clay body she usually used (Howell Stoneware) lacked elasticity and was subject to thermal shock. At this point, she decided to scrap her recipe and use the Delaware Studio Body.

To bring out the characteristics of unfired moist clay in the glaze-fired ware, Coffman used a yellow-gold slip in combination with a synthetic ash glaze sprayed on bisqueware. A trailing glaze was also used some-

Teapot, 5¼ inches in height, wheel thrown from Delaware Studio Body, with Synthetic Green Ash Glaze and a blue variation of Coleman Trailing Glaze, fired in reduction to cone 10–11.

Teapot, 5½ inches in height, white stoneware, with Yellow-Gold Slip and white trailing glaze, fired to cone 10–11 in reduction.

25

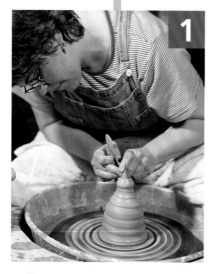

Coffman's teapot bodies are thrown without a bottom by opening all the way to the wheel head.

The body is altered by dropping and paddling, then a slab base is attached and the join smoothed with a roller.

Placement of the spout determines the pot's gesture.

A stopper with a curled knob comes next.

A handle is pulled directly from the teapot body.

After the pot is bisqued, designs are trailed in slip and glaze is sprayed overall.

times to give texture to smooth surfaces and direct the eye to significant
aspects of the form.

Further variations in surface were
developed in the firing. The pieces
were reduction fired either to cone
10 in a gas kiln or to cone 11 in a
wood kiln.

Developing this new work, from
clay preparation through forming,
assembling, glazing and firing, was
both a humbling and exhilarating
experience for Coffman. There is a
rhythm to the process of coming to
know one's medium. She has faith
in the rhythm of her art and life.
Spirited pots, celebrating art, cel-
ebrate life.

Lidded vessel, 9½
inches in height,
thrown and altered
Delaware Studio
Body, with Synthetic
Titanium Ash Glaze,
fired to cone 10–11 in
reduction, by Rebecca
Coffman, Hunting-
ton, Indiana.

Bottles, to 5 inches in height, white stoneware with Yellow-
Gold Slip, and blue and white trailing glaze, wood fired.

# Recipes

## Delaware Studio Body

Cone 10–11

| | |
|---|---|
| Custer Feldspar | 5 lb |
| A. P. Green Fireclay | 20 |
| Cedar Heights Goldart | 20 |
| Cedar Heights Redart | 20 |
| Kentucky Ball Clay (OM 4) | 15 |
| Mullite (48 mesh) | 2–5 |
| | 82–85 lb |

## Howell Stoneware Body

Cone 10–11

| | |
|---|---|
| Custer Feldspar | 5 lb |
| Cedar Heights Goldart | 40 |
| Cedar Heights Redart | 10 |
| Hawthorne Bond | 15 |
| Kentucky Ball Clay (OM 4) | 25 |
| Silica | 15 |
| Mullite (48 mesh) | 5 |
| | 115 lb |

## Yellow-Gold Slip

Cone 10–11

| | |
|---|---|
| Soda Ash | 1 % |
| Nepheline Syenite | 60 |
| EPK Kaolin | 39 |
| | 100 % |
| Add: Titanium Dioxide | 5 % |

## Coleman Trailing Glaze

Cone 10–11

| | |
|---|---|
| Talc | 10 % |
| Custer Feldspar | 70 |
| Kentucky Ball Clay (OM 4) | 20 |
| | 100 % |

## Synthetic Ash Glaze

Cone 10–11

| | |
|---|---|
| Bone Ash | 4 % |
| Magnesium Carbonate | 7 |
| Soda Ash | 4 |
| Whiting | 37 |
| Custer Feldspar | 26 |
| EPK Kaolin | 11 |
| Silica | 11 |
| | 100 % |

Apply by spraying, thin to moderately thick, depending on the amount of running desired. Color variations are possible with the following additions:

*Natural Ash:*

| | |
|---|---|
| Manganese Dioxide | 3.0% |
| Red Iron Oxide | 1.3% |

*Titanium Ash:*

| | |
|---|---|
| Titanium Oxide | 5 % |

*Dark Blue Ash:*

| | |
|---|---|
| Cobalt Carbonate | 1 % |
| Copper Carbonate | 3 % |

*Green Ash:*

| | |
|---|---|
| Copper Carbonate | 5 % |

# Ewer Bizarre
## Down with Round Brown

*by Annie Chrietzberg*

Students often flounder once they get past centering and opening—hypnotized, I'm convinced, by the ever-widening spiral. As a way to get around looking at the same bowls for such a long time, here's an assignment that's sure to start students on a journey into the realm of form. This assignment starts with the class standing up and shouting, "Down with round brown!", then we discuss parameters. The wheel may be used to create part of the piece, but the orientation of what comes off the wheel

must be changed. For spice, we mix an exploration of texture into the recipe. Advanced throwing skills are not required.

### A Basic Form

Here's how I made some recent ewers (I also use a similar set of instructions to make the 'furniture' these pots sit on). Throw a bottomless ring and pull it up at least four inches high. I usually make 8 to 12 of these pieces at a time near the end of the day. Start with something between 6 to 8 inches in diameter—it should be big enough to get your hands in, but not so big that you become bogged down with technical considerations, such as supports and drying schedules. I put deep ridges in my thrown rings, but you can create any texture you wish.

With a needle tool, make a line to follow later when cutting. Next, use a sponge to drizzle water into the ring so that when you use the cutting wire, it pulls the water with it,

"Trick Poodle Ewer," 8 inches in height. Variations are endless with this basic form.

"Ewer Bizarre," 9 inches in height, fired to cone 7 flat in an electric kiln then cooled to 1500°F and held for 30 minutes, which encourages microcrystalline activity in some of the glazes used.

Throw a bottomless ring and pull it up to the desired height. Rib or create texture as desired.

Use a needle tool to make a cut-off line while the ring is still round.

Drizzle water into the center and slide a cut-off wire, dragging the water under the walls.

Push the ring from the outside with a dowel, while supporting the inside with your hand.

Cut along the line and remove the rim. Gently reform the curve if necessary.

Make a slab and smooth it with a soft rib.

allowing the walls to float a bit and to move freely. After cutting the ring from the wheelhead, use a dowel to move the clay. The dowel provides even pressure and movement from top to bottom. Clean up the bat, removing traces of the original ring and all the water, then lightly cover the altered ring with plastic and allow it to set up overnight.

The next day I uncover the altered rings and pair them up (if I'm mak-ing oil and vinegar sets), and discard any shapes that aren't interesting. I pound out and texture the slabs with a specific orientation for the pattern I have in mind, making extra copies of each. That way, when I'm setting up the sides, if I make a mistake with orientation of pattern and cut incorrectly, I have another copy ready. Next, I cut off the rim. The rim can either be discarded or saved and added later to create a be-

Carefully lay the slab on a textured surface. Apply cornstarch to the surface to prevent sticking.

Roll the slab onto the texture carefully and evenly. Then lift it off and set aside.

Score deeply, apply slip, then score and slip again to create a definite interface.

Transfer the shape of the rim to the textured slab by placing the slab on the rim.

Remove the slab and cut outside of the slip line. Remove the excess clay.

Shape, score and apply slip to the slab, then place it on the form.

zel effect on and around the textured slab. When making numerous pieces to assemble, monitor them carefully. As they become dry enough to handle without distortion, wrap them in plastic or place them in plastic boxes with damp sponges to keep them in their workable state.

To assemble, score deeply, apply slip, then score and slip again to create a definite interface between the pieces you're joining. The key to

creating pots that look fresh rather than belabored is to handle them as little as possible. I only touch the wet, malleable clay when necessary. For example, if I need to turn a piece over, rather than picking it up with my hands, I have a wide selection of foam pads and wareboards that I use to flip them. If I damage a piece while handling it, I also have a selection of cheap pencil erasers that I can sand into appropriate curves

Nudge the slab into place and press down on it while smoothing the sides.

Cut off the bat, protect the texture with foam, place a bat on top, then flip the form over.

Cut off the rim and attach the second side using the same method as before.

For the spout, create a textured slab. Place a template on slab and cut around it at an angle.

Score edges, then lift the sides and roll them over, pushing against the scored edge.

Press the overlap together, support the inside with your finger and apply light pressure.

that I use to remove tool marks and nicks from wet clay.

## Slab Spouts

Spouts made with slabs have distinctly different qualities than thrown ones. In general, slab-made spouts can be more expressive, sculptural and precise than typical thrown spouts. Templates are a very important tool for form development because you can work with the same shape over and over again, which allows you to explore variables such as the thickness of the slab, the reaction of different textures to being bent, different ways of cutting, such as bevels and darts, and different degrees of alteration. Another benefit of working with templates is that with a little attention and minimal record keeping, you'll learn how to change two-dimensional shapes to accommodate what you desire in three-dimensional forms.

Use a tool or finger to blend the inside seam and shape the spout from the inside.

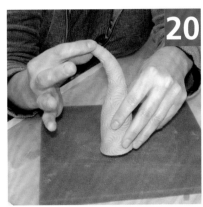

Bend the spout using light pressure.

Hold the spout up to the form and trace the silhouette of the form onto the spout.

Cut half the spout off, then turn it over and place it on the other half of the spout.

Trace around the reversed first half, then cut the remaining half.

Make final adjustments, then hold the spout in place to mark the opening.

I use old file folders or card stock for templates. For a spout, figure out the rough shape of your template on a piece of scratch paper, then fold it in half. Create a crease in the card stock and trace the shape onto it. Cut out the template. You can re-cut templates that don't quite work, and every time you create one for a spout, make a quick, exploratory example with clay. Don't join the seam, just scan the piece for correct volume.

Mark directly on the clay where you need more or less volume. Unroll the spout and compare it with the template, removing some volume from the existing one, or make a new one if more volume is needed. Using a template with pleasing lines and curves is the first step in the direction of making a nice spout.

A common question potters ask the first time they see someone make a slab spout is "How do you get them to

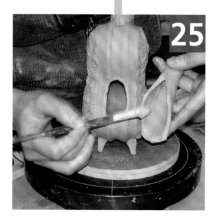

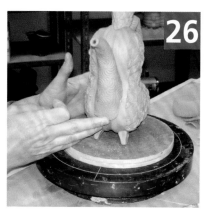

Cut the opening ¼ inch inside the line, then score and slip both pieces and attach.

Use light pressure at the very edge of the texture to join the parts.

Detail of Ewer Bizarre.

be round?" The answer is an appropriately thin slab, correct beveling of edges and lots of practice. If you can dedicate a large chunk of time—say, half a day—to just cutting out and making slab spouts over and over, I guarantee the last spout of your session will be more elegant than your first!

I always have card stock and scissors close at hand for making and adjusting templates. I use both textured and smooth slabs, depending on the pots I'm making. And I've made slab spouts of every size, from tiny ewers up to big watering cans. I use very wet clay when making spouts, and a piece of egg-crate foam helps keep the spout from rolling over and collapsing if I need some set up time for larger spouts. Remember to keep those fingers clean! The tiniest of crumbs show up when you bend a thin slab of clay all the way around to form a truncated cone!

The actual pouring edge and hole of every spout is arguably its most important part, both visually and functionally. Does the size of the hole relate properly to the viscosity of the liquid being poured through it? Is it a nice even shape? The shape of the hole makes an instant impression on the eye. Is there a suitable edge along the bottom of the hole that will clip the stream and prevent drips when the pot is returned to its upright position? Some people who make slab spouts pinch the business end of the slab before rolling it into a spout. That certainly works, but currently, my preferred method is to do a little bit of sanding with emery cloth once the piece is bone dry. I prefer emery cloth to sand paper, because it rips in straight lines and can be smoothly rolled into a tiny abrasive cylinder to shape the actual hole in the spout. I am able to get very precise results this way.

# Altered Shapes

*by Gabriel Brubacher*

**Gestural teapot, 8 inches in height, Shino with ash, cone 10 reduction.**

My approach to ceramics begins with throwing simple forms on the wheel, then altering them to create a desired effect. Using the same approach while teaching, I instruct students to create a basic cylinder, and then manipulate it to create unique shapes and forms, which soon start to reflect the students' personalities. Altering cylinders by faceting, cutting, darting and elongating shortly after learning to throw helps students find ways to communicate an idea, and to decide what process works best for them. Here's a simple way to alter and give a new look to a vase form. This straightforward approach includes three basic ideas: create the form, alter the contour and make the cylinder oval. These steps are open to many interpretations and experimentation is encouraged. With a few extra steps, it's easy to turn this vase form into a teapot, pitcher, basket or covered jar.

**Bread Basket, 10 inches in length, Shino with ash, cone 10 reduction.**

Center and open to the wheel head (figure 1). Throw the cylinder to the desired height (figure 2). Use a rib to clean the walls of the cylinder (figure 3). As the cylinder turns, push out from the inside with a rubber rib (figure 4). Draw a line with a dull pointed tool on the outside just below the rib to accentuate the movement (figure 5). Repeat this motion a second time. You can decide if you would like the lines to emulate each other. After developing the contour, cut the form from the wheel (figure 6).

Once the form is free, distort it into an oval starting at the bottom (figure 7). The extent of distortion is up to you. Allow the form to set up (I let mine set up overnight). Roll out or throw a slab and place it onto the wheel. Score the form and slab (figure 8). Attach the cylinder by pressing and smoothing the bottom edge into the slab (figure 9). Cut and remove the excess clay (figure 10). Bevel the edge and use a sponge to clean the connection. Use a rubber rib to clean and create a concaved bottom (figure 11).

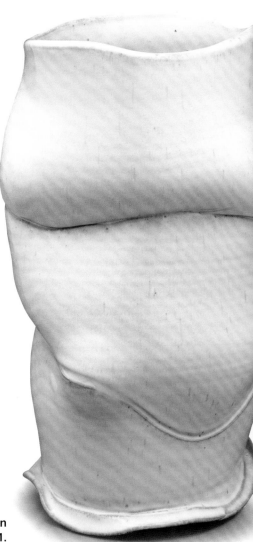

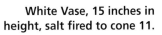
White Vase, 15 inches in
height, salt fired to cone 11.

Ash Vase, 14 inches
in height, salt fired
to cone 11.

Oil and Vinegar set,
5 inches in height,
Shino with ash,
cone 10 reduction.

# No-Measure Lids

*by Doug Gray*

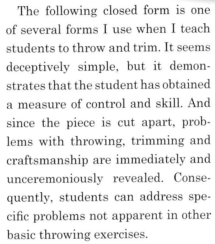

L earning to throw is challenging—from the initial struggle to center, to establishing height and thin even walls. There's an ever-present desire to control the profile of the form, and to alter its direction and contour as it emerges from the lump of freshly wedged clay.

Mastering some forms comes easier than mastering others. For example, clay tends to expand as it's thinned and thrown taller. And the movement of the clay responding from centrifugal force and the friction of the hand subtly exerting itself against the clay wall factor in to why bowl forms are usually easier to achieve than cylinders or closed forms.

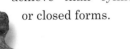

The following closed form is one of several forms I use when I teach students to throw and trim. It seems deceptively simple, but it demonstrates that the student has obtained a measure of control and skill. And since the piece is cut apart, problems with throwing, trimming and craftsmanship are immediately and unceremoniously revealed. Consequently, students can address specific problems not apparent in other basic throwing exercises.

Don't misunderstand me. This form is more than just a teaching tool. I've enjoyed making these small containers for years. It's a fast and easy method for creating lidded forms without calipers or measurements of any kind. And the best part is that the lids fit perfectly each and every time.

## Throwing

Center approximately one pound of clay (figure 1). More could be used for larger round forms, but I prefer to keep these containers small and jewel-like. Open the clay and leave $^3/_8$ inch of clay on the bottom for a trimmed foot (figure 2). Slightly

Three examples illustrating the variety of lid contours available with this technique. Fast and easy to do, these forms also are a great learning tool because cutting the lid reveals any problems with throwing, trimming and craftsmanship.

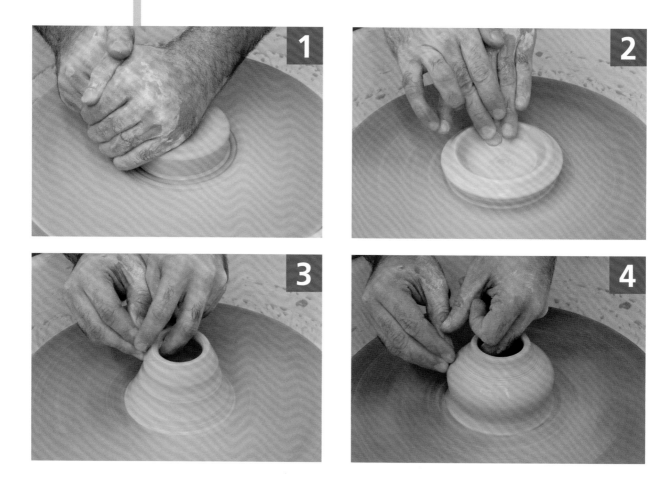

curve the bottom to establish the contour of the entire form. Exert more pressure with the outside hand and throw a slight conical shape (figure 3). This makes the form much easier to close later. Keep the rim open only wide enough to get a couple of fingers inside. Leave a thick bead of clay at the rim. A thicker rim is beneficial both for closing the form and creating a knob. Once the height is established and the clay wall thinned sufficiently, round the form by exerting more pressure from the inside (figure 4). Maintain some support with the outside hand so the form remains centered and doesn't twist. If the base is too thin or over extended the form could collapse later. A lot of torque is placed on the form when closing the rim and fashioning the knob.

Push through the thick bead of clay at the rim to close the form (figure 5). Keep a finger or two inside the form to support the clay wall while you close. If your fingers are too big, try using a pencil or handle of a tool. To facilitate drying and deter S-cracks, remove any water that might remain in the bottom of the form before you close it completely. The opening eventually becomes small enough to squeeze shut com-

pletely (figure 6). A short column of clay should be preserved from the rim to aid this motion. Keep your fingers very wet as you compress the rim from both sides to prevent the rim from twisting. Fashion a knob from the excess clay by applying pressure from the top and support from the side (figure 7).

Undercut the knob slightly using the rounded end of a tool for a more dramatic profile (figure 8). This makes the knob easier to grasp once glazed and fired. Use a soft flexible rib to refine the overall form (figure 9). Because the form is closed, air trapped inside acts as a

support, keeping the form from collapsing even under rather aggressive shaping. Remove the piece from the wheel and place on a ware board to dry. Poke a small hole in the form with a needle tool to allow the air to escape while the piece dries and begins to shrink.

## Trimming

At the leather-hard stage, place the piece in a bisque-fired chuck (figure 10). Chucks are useful for trimming forms that are uneven or fragile, or cannot be turned upside down on the wheel. Thrown chucks may be used in either the green or bisque state. Since clay doesn't stick well to bisqueware, soak the bisqued chuck in water for several minutes before using to make the clay wads hold more securely. To level the piece, hold a needle tool steady as it revolves (figure 11). The needle marks the highest spot. Shift the piece in the chuck until it is level and the needle makes an even mark around the bottom. Secure the form to the chuck with wads of soft clay (figure 12). Apply only enough pressure to stick the wads to both the piece and the chuck. The piece should not shift in the chuck.

Center the chuck by holding the needle tool to the side of the form to mark the side that protrudes farthest from the center. Align the mark so that it faces you and push the chuck away from you slightly. Repeat this until an even mark is made around the piece. Use additional wads of soft clay to secure the chuck to the wheel head (figure 13). Again, be careful not to push the chuck off center as you do this.

As the interior of the piece cannot be seen at this point, it's important to visualize the inner curve you established while opening and throwing the form. Trim the bottom of the form, creating a foot ring (figure 14). Mirror the exterior contour off of the visualized memory of the interior contour. Tapping the form and comparing the sounds produced at various points indicates if the thickness of the clay wall is consistent. Turn the form right side up in the chuck. Level as before and use a needle tool to score two faint concentric circles (figure 15). These circles facilitate both the design and ultimate removal of the lid. So, carefully consider their placement in terms of visual proportions and adequate access to the interior.

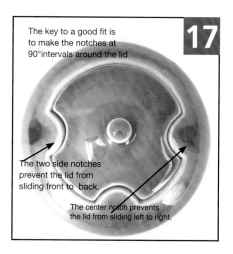

The key to a good fit is to make the notches at 90° intervals around the lid

The two side notches prevent the lid from sliding front to back.

The center notch prevents the lid from sliding left to right.

## Cutting

Rather than cutting a circular lid that slides around on the form, draw a modified, notched lid with the aid of a round plastic form (figure 16). The smaller, or top concentric circle establishes a uniform height for each of the arcs. The arcs and the larger, or bottom, circle determines where the lid will be cut from the base. Looking down on the lid from the top (figure 17), trace the two rounded arcs on opposite sides of the form, at 3 and 9 o'clock respectively. Place a third arc between the other two at

6 o'clock. The notches are located at 90° intervals around the circumference of the circle to prevent the lid from slipping either right to left or front to back. Two notches would be sufficient, but add a third to visually balance the composition. Add more notches of varying sizes and shapes if desired. Remember, however, the more complex the pattern, the more difficult it becomes for the user to orient and replace the lid during use.

Holding a thin knife blade at a 45° angle, cut the lid from the form (figure 18). The cut runs along the larger, or bottom circle, and continues along each of the three arcs. Once cut, the notches in the lid create a proper seat and prevent sliding. The lid fits perfectly every time, even without measurements and calipers. Smooth unwanted score lines, crumbs and sharp edges or corners with a wet finger or sponge. These areas tend to trap glaze, even when waxed over, and these droplets of glaze can be enough to fuse the lid shut during firing.

# Taming the Dragon
## Large Sprigged Pots

*by Alan Frewin*

Dragon imagery is present in many different cultures. Although the depictions of these beasts vary in design, all are immediately recognizable as dragons. I decided that these creatures would be a fun addition to my large garden pots. After sketching and making a clay model of the dragon, I cast a plaster press mold. This took some time to create, but now I can "breed" dragons by the score. My large dragons are intended for large pots, but small ones look good on lamp bases, vases, deep-sided bowls and tiles, and the same process applies.

## Making the pot

When making a new design, determine how big the pot will be when it is dry and ready to go into the kiln. Since clay shrinks as it dries, make a pot as large as is practical to fit nicely into the kiln. It is easier to throw a large pot in sections. Draw the shape of the pot on graph paper and mark where you want the two sections to join.

For the pot I'm demonstrating here, I used 22 pounds of clay for the first section, which will be 11 inches wide at the base, 11 inches tall and 18½ inches in diameter measuring from the outside edges (figure 1). Make the central drain hole while opening the pot and leave it attached to the bat. Allow the section to dry until it is firm enough to bear the weight of the second section. To help it firm up evenly, put some wet rags around the top rim. For the second section, I used 20 pounds of clay and opened it as a ring. The first section will have shrunk a little as it firmed up, so you'll need to measure the diameter from the center of each rim. Throw the ring to about 6 inches in height leaving plenty of clay at the bottom (this will form the top rim of the finished pot). Draw the top of the ring out until it is the same diameter as the top of the first section (figure 2). Make an indent in the rim for the first section to fit into. Remove the ring (still on its bat) from the wheel and put the first section back onto the wheel. Center it, then score or rough up the rim, and spread on some slip.

Turn the top section over. With a large pot, this is best done with a swinging up and over motion (figure 3). Tip: Practice the movement first using a bat. When moving large or heavy pots it pays to know exactly how and where they are to be placed—better safe than sorry. Place the top section onto the bottom section (figure 4) and give the bat a few gentle taps to settle it down. Smooth the two sections together with a damp sponge.

Cut the bat from the top with a wire (figure 5). Keep the wire close to the bat for a nice clean cut. Smooth the inside join with a sponge and a steel kidney. Round off the rim and throw the ring up until the pot is 19 inches high with an outside diameter of 21 inches (figure 6). When doing this step, throw slightly higher than the finished size because you'll lose some height once the pot is opened out to its final diameter. A steel kidney is very useful for smoothing and getting a nice curve on the outside of the pot. Allow the pot to dry slowly until it's firm, but still a little tacky to the touch. This provides a good surface for the dragon to hold onto. Do not cut or remove the completed form from the bat until after the dragon is applied.

## Making the Model and the Mold

Make a full-size drawing of the dragon on paper and cut it out. Find a flat board, and lay a plastic sheet on top that's flexible and thick enough to not wrinkle or lift as you work. Lay the paper cut-out on the board. Make sure there is at least 2 inches of board all the way around the paper. Next, outline the cut-out with a permanent marker.

Start building your model dragon with clay. Make sure the model does not have any undercuts because, if it does, you will not be able to pull it out of the plaster mold without damaging it. The quickest way to get rid of small undercuts is to fill them with fairly thick slip using a slip trailer, repeating several times until they are all filled in.

You can make dragon scales by pressing the flat side of a round-end modeling tool into the clay. For better definition, starting at the tail end, press very small uniform balls of clay into the body with a slightly dampened modeling tool. Vary the size of the scales—small at the tail end and bigger as you proceed to the main body. You will get undercuts as you make the dragon's scales but they can be filled as described above.

When the model is completed, build a wall around it that extends at least 1 inch above the highest part of the dragon. If you use wooden boards you will have a straight-sided mold. If your dragon has a number of steep curves, you can make the mold lighter by following the shape using flexible plastic or, aluminum strips, clipped at the top and stuck down at the bottom with clay on the outside (see below). Make sure that the walls are held

firmly in place and are able to contain the liquid plaster without falling apart. Now paint around the dragon and the inside of the containing wall with a good coating of liquid household soap to stop the plaster from sticking to those parts. Do not get soap on the dragon.

Mix your plaster. Have a bowl of water with approximately the same volume of water as the space to fill in the mold—better to overestimate a little. Sprinkle the powdered plaster in the water until it stops sinking and begins to show above the water. Now put your hand into the bowl (wear thin, protective gloves and a respirator) and gently agitate the mix making sure there are no lumps. Starting at one corner, pour the plaster into the mold. When the dragon is covered, put your hand palm-down into the liquid plaster and make a gentle up-and-down pumping motion to force any air bubbles to the surface, and ensure that there are no missed areas. To make a good, strong mold and allow for plenty of water absorption, the plaster level needs to be about 1 inch above the highest part of the dragon. If you find that you have underestimated the amount of plaster and the plaster in the mold is beginning to set, quickly score the setting plaster, mix up some more, and then add it to the mold.

After the plaster sets, gently remove the containing wall. Turn the mold over, remove the board and peel off the plastic sheet. Pull the model dragon out of the mold by gently pressing a ball of clay onto it and pulling from the edges. Do not use any of the waste clay that may contain bits of plaster to make pots—best to throw it away. When the mold is completely dry, take it outside and sand off the sharp outside edges. Clean out the mold by taking a ball of clay and pressing it into the mold to remove any residue and loose bits of plaster. Tip: When dry, you can paint a coat of fiberglass onto the top flat edges of the mold to protect it when scraping away surplus clay. Check online, the Yellow Pages, or a boating supply store for fiberglass products.

## Making a dragon

Make a good-sized sausage of clay—fairly soft will shrink a little more than very firm clay and is easier to get out of the mold. Start at the head of the dragon mold and press clay from the center to the edges making sure that all the air is pushed out (figure 7). Overfill the mold, and thump the clay down with the edge of your hand from head to tail and back again. Drag a wire across the top of the mold to remove surplus clay (figure 8), then smooth by dragging a straight-edged wooden tool across the mold (figure 9). Wipe away any clay from the top of the mold with a damp sponge.

Some parts of the dragon are quite thick and, when combined with the thickness of the pot, some cracking can occur during the firing. To avoid this, scoop out some of the clay (figure 10). Pierce holes in the underside with a needle tool to let air to escape during the firing. Allow the clay to set up for twenty minutes or until the edges of the dragon are shrinking away from the edges of the mold. Gently ease the dragon loose from the mold using a small lump of clay (figure 11). Work your way along the edges first. Then, working from head to tail, free the main body. A slight twisting movement will unstick the clay from the dragon.

Place sticks of wood on each side of the mold and lay a board on top (figure 12). Flip the mold and board over with an upward and over swinging movement. The dragon will drop from the mold and onto the board.

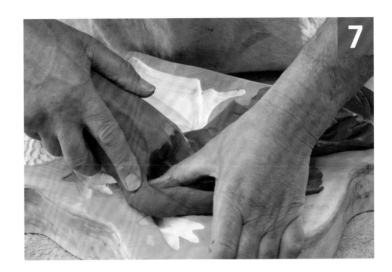

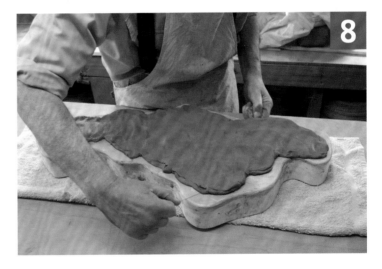

## Applying the dragon

It is not possible to pick up a large dragon with your hands and adhere it to a pot without damaging the fine detail, but it is easier with a sponge support. Get a piece of sponge a bit bigger than the dragon and about 1½ inches thick. Glue on some half-inch-thick strips of sponge to stop the dragon from sliding while being pressed onto the pot. Lay the sponge support on the dragon and, holding the sponge and board together, flip it over. The dragon is now lying upside down on the sponge (figure 13). With a slip trailer and a flat 1-inch brush, apply slip thickly onto the dragon with a dabbing or patting motion (figure 14). Make sure that the whole dragon is covered, particularly fine edges like pointed claws.

Your dragon will look livelier if he has some upward movement, as if moving up the pot with his head fairly near the top. Pick up the sponge and, holding at the correct angle, push and wrap him around the pot (figure 15). Hold for a moment to make sure that he will not slide off. Put the sponge support aside, and now working from his middle, use a soft sponge to press him firmly home. As you press outward you will see some of the slip being squeezed out—this is good. Make sure that all the fine-pointed extremities are firmly attached and wipe away any surplus slip.

If you are feeling adventurous when your dragon is finished, try carving or scratching swirling pat-

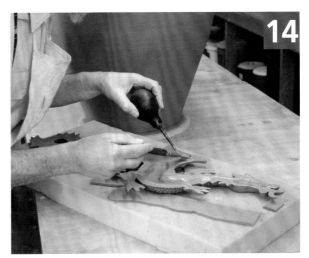

terns onto the rest of the pot (figure 16). This will raise some hard, rough edges. Leave them alone until the pot is nearly dry and brush them away with a suede shoe brush. Dry your dragon pot very, very slowly. Keep it away from drafts and direct sunlight, and cover with an old sheet. If you dry him out too fast, you risk cracks and distorting because the pot has more clay on the dragon side, which can cause uneven drying.

# Throwing Tall Narrow Forms

*by Annie Robbins*

**Three tall bottles (the middle one is 27 inches high) that began as tall narrow cylinders. Annie Robbins states "Lucie Rie is the potter I most admire and emulate."**

I've always favored tall narrow forms, but no matter how hard I've tried, getting anything over 18 to 20 inches high just eluded me. Then a few years ago, I sprained my right wrist and thumb in a car accident so I didn't work for a while to give my hand a rest. Fearing the worst, I went to a hand specialist and broke into tears. He explained that hand injuries were sometimes worse for artists because we use our hands to express ourselves. He encouraged me to "find a new way" and inspired me to challenge myself. After years of hard work as a thrower and even longer as a very stubborn woman, I left his office baffled.

Somehow I had to take the stress of pulling up tall pieces off my right hand and wrist, and although I hardly expected to come out ahead, I was hoping to break even. The result is that I discovered a technique that allowed me to stretch beyond my previous limits. I'm sure other potters have worked this way, but for me it's still new and exciting!

## Tips for Success

- Apply the seven basic "C's" for throwing: Collar it in, Clean it up/off, Cut it off, Compress, Compress, Compress and, of course, Cheat whenever possible.

- Tall narrow forms can quickly become off center, similar to the rope in a spinning lasso. The faster the wheel spins, the more exaggerated the twirl. Work at a reasonable pace, and when in doubt, SLOW DOWN and collar your piece.

- Water is not your best friend when throwing these tall forms. Water weakens the piece and lessens the integrity of the clay's strength, so use it sparingly. Tip: Throughout the throwing process, I usually wet my hand instead of the clay

## Process

Begin with well-wedged small balls of clay (figure 1). Form a large centered mass that's tall and narrow (figure 2). Open the centered clay burrowing your left hand into the mass using very little water (figure 3). Lift your hand out while opening your fingers inside the piece and raise it slowly so the opening is no more than about 4 inches across. Clean off excess moisture on the outside with a metal rib (figure 4). If there is any unevenness at the top of the piece, use a needle tool to trim it off (figure 5). Do not press the unevenness back into the piece.

Now, get ready to cone the clay. A similar technique is used by many potters when centering. The way that works best for my right wrist is to place my palm at 12 o'clock, flat against the piece facing my stomach, fingers aiming in a counterclockwise direction (figure 6). My left wrist is bent back at 6 o'clock, fingers pointing clockwise. Compress, using the weight of your center, and slowly bring the piece up while gradually collaring the cylinder (figure 7). There should be some friction against the counter-clockwise motion of the clay. While compressing your hands together, move them clockwise to the 3 and 9 o'clock positions (figure 8). With a wheelhead speed of about 60 rpm, this collaring action should take only about 3 to 4 seconds. The compression will make the opening smaller. That's ok for now.

Clean off the outside of the piece with a metal rib, open the top a little and cut off any excess at the top (figure 9). Repeat the collaring process at least once more (figure 10). Metal ribs tend to scrape off excess slip as opposed to rubber ribs, which compress the clay and moisture together. Wet your left hand and arm and insert them while opening your fingers just a little on the way down because the opening is now narrow from the collaring (figure 11). The collaring compressed the walls of the cylinder and made them thicker, but this left compression marks on the inside of the form, which you can feel as the wheel rotates. Use the whole long length of the outside of your thumb and apply pressure in the opposite direction of your wheel's counter-clockwise rotation (go from 3 to 5 o'clock). As you insert your arm down into the cylinder, use this motion as an opportunity to compress the walls from the inside (figure 12). With the exception of the moisture on your hands and arm, there should

be no need for any additional moisture on the inside of the piece. While this step usually lowers the height, the cylinder is still over my elbow! Clean and trim the form (figure 13). Already, you should have a nice tall narrow cylinder, and you're ready to make your first pull.

Stretch your wet hand and arm down to the base. Compress the thumb side of your left hand to the wall and start to pull up (figure 14).

It's hard to get much strength without a bent elbow but don't worry about the thickness of your piece at the base because it needs to be thick to hold up the walls. It also needs to be thick so that, when your piece is finished, it has some weight at the base so the cat doesn't knock it over. Remember, you can always trim it off later if you want. The form will twist as you work your way to the top. Since the clay is not distributed

the same way as it is on a wide piece, it usually takes me three passes to complete one pull. Here's how: Pull up about one-third from the base (figure 15). Right before you sense the twist is near, withdraw your hand. Now, place your hands at 3 and 9 o'clock, directly above the place where you stopped pulling (one-third from the base) (figure 16) and start to collar it

in, bringing your hands up as you go (figure 17). Clean off the piece and trim the top. Note: When I pull, I use a damp sponge on the outside in my right hand. The piece will be hugging your left arm so, if the moisture runs out, be ready to squeeze some water down your arm.

Invert your wet left hand and arm back into the cylinder and go down

**(Left)** "The Necklace," 19¾ inches in height. Annie fires all her pieces in an oxidation atmosphere and often fires them multiple times.

**(Middle)** One of Annie's favorites is the bottle form with a cup shape on top. This is a tricky form since it is all thrown as one piece.

**(Right)** Annie allows the lips to speak for themselves and in this way the forms find their own voice.

to the area you started collaring (not lower) (figure 18). Compress and pull up until you feel the piece may want to twist, around two-thirds of the way up (figure 19). Remove your hand and repeat the collaring process from the two-thirds point (figure 20). Cut excess off the top and clean with a metal rib. Insert wet hand and arm down just as far as you last started collaring (at the two-thirds point) and pull to the top and trim the rim. Note: If you compress too hard when you collar the piece, the area above your hands may want to spin like a lasso. The taller the section, the more likely this is to happen.

The next step is difficult and requires terrific coordination between your foot pedal and the speed of your hands. Start at the base and quickly collar up all the way (figures 21). Sometimes, I apply water directly to the piece before this pass. The hand-foot coordination is similar to speeding on a country road—the faster you're traveling, the quicker you need to twist and turn with the curves. You'll know right away if your hands aren't fast enough because the piece will spin out of control.

One fun way to deal with this problem is to recruit a friend! Have that person stand directly across from you (figure 22). Make sure her or his hands are wet. Have your friend place their hands on either side of the cylinder at 9 and 3 o'clock positions, thumbs up about 2 to 3 inches from the top. Be ready for your next motion because if you wait too long her hands could dry from friction. If this person is not a potter, explain they aren't squeezing, just "spotting" your piece. Collar the form while compressing and raise your hands at a fairly swift pace (figure 23). If my wheel is traveling at 60 rpm, I generally cover the whole upward distance in 4 to 5 revolutions. Be sure to have your friend move her hands up if she feels the piece moving up.

Now clean off the piece with your metal rib, trim the excess, and you should have a nice tall cylinder. This is where the fun begins, so start to create your form (figure 24).

# Pulling Long Handles

*by Kathy Chamberlin*

I have found that the addition of long, hand-pulled clay handles, along with the decorative knots, to my basket forms has helped me to develop my own personal style. The inspiration is derived from traditional Chinese and Japanese woven baskets. I hope my demonstration of this technique helps you to improve your handles and enhance your personal style.

Currently, I am producing a series of baskets using bowl shapes and tall, cylindrical vessels. This is a method I have developed for pulling long handles and attaching them to my forms. The handle structure that I use closely resembles a catenary arch, a curve theoretically formed by hanging a perfectly flexible and inextensible cord of uniform density and cross section, freely, from two fixed points.

I work with a white stoneware and fire to cone 10 in reduction, but the following steps could be used for any clay body or firing range. Each clay body reacts differently and some experimentation needs to be done. It's very important to use a highly plastic clay so that the handles maintain their integrity through all steps— pulling, shaping, drying and attaching. I use clay reprocessed from scraps, trimmings and throwing slip. This clay seems to have more plasticity, possibly because of the fine particles that have collected, the aging process and adequate water content.

When pulling the handle, you need to make sure there are no air pockets, surface cracks, or hard and soft areas in the clay. Any problems will show up in the bisque or glaze firings, and the clay handles will not maintain their shape or integrity.

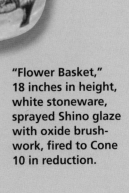

**"Flower Basket,"
18 inches in height,
white stoneware,
sprayed Shino glaze
with oxide brush-
work, fired to Cone
10 in reduction.**

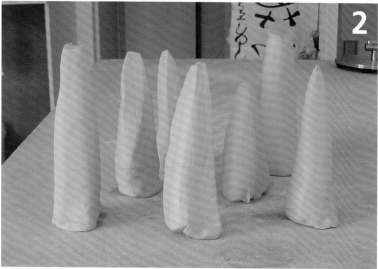

## Process

I throw two basic shapes for my baskets—cylinders from 8 to 12 inches tall, and bowls from 4 to 8 inches tall, each with a span up to 9 inches in diameter (figure 1). With larger diameters, these handles have a tendency to distort or fall during firing. I shape well-wedged clay into carrotlike forms for pulling the handles (figure 2), making sure I have enough clay for the size of the handle I want to make. Extra clay is needed in order to hold the clay while pulling the handle.

Hold the clay at the top with one hand while pulling the handle with the other (figure 3). Using a continuous stroking motion, wet your hand before each pull. Compress the clay with even pressure from top to bottom (figure 4). The structure of your hand and its position during each pull determines the handle's shape. Practice helps you find the best position for your hand and the proper amount of pressure to apply. Use your thumb down the center of the handle to define the shape.

I pull clay handles up to 30 inches long, let them hang straight down and dry very slowly (figure 5). Drying time depends on your local climate and environment. I do not recommend using direct sunlight, heat guns or fans to dry the handles. This can cause uneven drying and cracking during the shaping of the handle. After the handles start to stiffen, they can be shaped into the desired curves. You need to experiment to

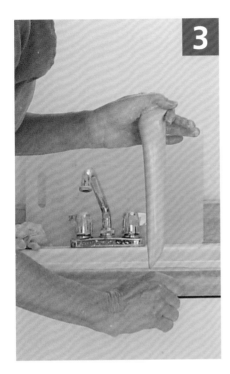

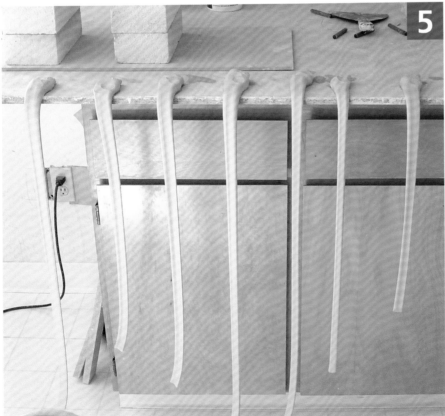

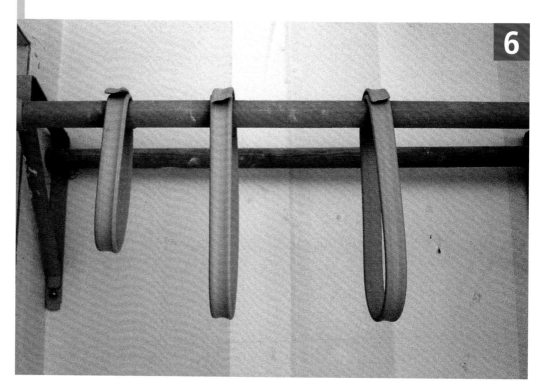

find the amount of time needed for your clay to dry before being shaped into the curved form. If it's too dry, it cracks, and if it's too wet, it will not hold its shape. Place over a wooden dowel rack (figure 6), but other curved items also can be used. It's important to continue drying the handle as evenly as possible. Test the clay by touch. It's ready to attach when the clay can hold its shape. The approximate time from pulling handles, shaping and attaching to a pot is about five hours.

When attaching clay handles, I build two level stands from bricks or blocks allowing me to work on the piece upside down (figure 7). This lets the handle hang and retain its curve while you score, slip and fasten the ends to the basket. When adding double-layer handles, I fas-

ten the bottom layer to the inside of the form and the top layer to the outside. There is a limited window of working time for this step.

I finish by adding decorative knots and cleaning the joined areas (figure 8). Then I cover with plastic to dry upside down. After a few days, I turn the basket over, inspect and touch up any details, then turn upside down and cover again so it will dry slowly and evenly.

I bisque fire the pots after they are completely dry. Instead of either dipping or pouring, I spray most of the glazes due to the fragile nature of the handles. I fire the pieces to cone 10 in a reduction atmosphere.

"Fruit Basket,"
18 inches in height,
white stoneware,
copper red glaze,
fired, fired to cone 10
in reduction.

# Making Tall Amphoras

*by Anderson Turner*

**Amphora, 42 inches in height, by Aaron Calvert. An amphora is a general name for a large ovoid jar made by the Greeks and Romans and identified by two loop handles. They were used for storing oil, wine or other liquids, or as prizes and ornaments.**

Amphoras are ancient Greek storage jars or vases with two handles, which rise almost to the level of the mouth of the pot. Many modern potters enjoy making these large forms in their own unique style. Kent State University (Ohio) ceramics professor Kirk Mangus makes large amphoras as part of his repertoire and enjoys using this ancient form as a vehicle

**"Kiss," 38 inches in height, wood fired, by Kirk Mangus. Amphoras used for food had pointed bases that were stuck into the ground for stability. When used as ornaments or given as prizes, amphoras were usually decorated and rested on bases.**

**Rim detail. When used for storage, amphoras were sometimes sealed with wood and smeared with pitch.**

to express his own sense of illustration and gesture. Aaron Calvert studied what Kirk taught him and developed it into something uniquely expressive of his own ideas. The following instructions will enable you to do the same.

## Throwing

Aaron makes large amphoras using six thrown sections, then arranging them in a planned sequence to form a large pot. The sections are base, lower center section, center section, upper center section, neck and rim.

Begin by throwing the center section of the pot. This section should be a wide cylinder with walls as straight as possible (figure 1). This part is done first so you can gauge the size to throw the upper and lower center sections and because it gives you a feel for what the overall size of the pot will be. Create a thin lip on the top of the center section so you have extra clay to aid in joining the sections together.

Throw the bottom center section. Using the center section as a guide, throw this piece with a base the same width as the center section. When completed, this piece should resemble an open dome (figure 2). You're throwing this section upside down, so the top will join with the base of the amphora. Add lines in the top of this section to aid in lining up with base during construction.

Throw the upper center section by repeating the same process as Step 2, except make the top of this piece slightly tapered (figure 3) so that

you have an easier time attaching the neck. Be sure to add lines on the top to aid with lining the pieces up during construction.

Throw the neck using the upper center section as a guide (figure 4), and with a base big enough to fit nicely over the lines you've drawn on the top of the upper center section. Make the neck as tall or as short as you want (this one is 9 inches tall). Also, be sure to make the top of the neck as flat as possible so that you can join it to the rim.

Throw the rim. This is basically a flat-bottomed bowl with sides that come up about four inches (figure 5). The walls can be straight up and down or even something new and different of your own creation. Aaron likes to make hard-edged walls that form a clean zigzag shape. Using the opening at the top of the neck as a guide, cut a hole in the center of the

base of the bowl. When you construct the pot, you will be flipping this bowl over and the hole will be the opening at the top of the completed amphora.

Use the bottom center section as a guide for the diameter of the base (figure 6). Create a V-shaped bowl with an opening big enough to accommodate the top of the bottom center section. Because this is the base of the amphora, make this section as sturdy as possible, depending on the size of the piece you've thrown.

## Construction

Begin by scoring and applying slip to the inside of the top of the base section (figure 7). Score and slip the top of the lower center section (figure 8). Flip the base section over and place it on the bottom center section (figure 9). Using your finger or a tool, smooth the sections together (figure 10). Attaching leather-hard pieces together by scoring and applying slip is called "luting." Release the lower center section from the throwing bat using a cut-off wire (figure 11). Flip the base/

"Dead," 20 inches in height, wood fired, by Kirk Mangus.

bottom center assembly and place it in the center of the wheelhead, then score and slip the top rim (figure 12). Score and slip the top of the center section, then flip it over and place it on top of the base assembly. Using the rim of extra clay you made, meld the center and base assembly together (figure 13). Score and slip what is now the top of the center section. Flip it over, then score and slip the bottom rim. Meld the sections together with your hands or with a rib (figure 14). Score and slip the top of the neck, then score and slip the inside of the rim (figure 15). Flip the neck over and attach it to the inside of the rim. Be sure to line up the neck with the hole you cut in the base of the rim (figure 16). Score and slip the inside of the bottom of the neck, then score and slip the top of the upper center section. Flip the neck/rim assembly over and attach it to the upper center section (figure 17). The neck should fit just over the top of the upper center section. Meld the sections together. If possible, meld the section together from the inside as well. Congratulations! You've made an amphora (figure 18)!

# Asymmetrical Handbuilding

*by Jim Connell*

**This teapot began with a slab base laid on a plywood pattern. Using thick coils, the form took shape quickly, and was ready for carving and finishing within a short time. Copper red carved form, 14 inches in length, stoneware, fired to cone 10 and sandblasted.**

I started throwing during my second semester in clay, and it's been a long love affair holding me in its grip ever since. For many years, I never thought about making clay forms any other way, and was content even though I knew the wheel had limitations. The wheel's main limitation (or attribute depending on which way you look at it) is its inevitable adherence to symmetry. No matter what shape is thrown, they're all even, round and symmetrical. Even when altered, paddled, sliced and darted, the forms still reveal the roots of their symmetrical origins.

I always felt secure living with this regularity, because it was easy to accept and difficult to avoid. Still, thoughts of working off the central axis began to surface. I wasn't sure how to make the transition to asymmetry because for years I wasn't able to even consider handbuilding. The handbuilding process always seemed too tedious and time consuming for my temperament—it lacked excitement, and it wasn't magical enough.

This prejudice changed when I attended a workshop given at a local college where Sally Brogden was running a hands-on handbuilding

workshop. I dropped in two hours after the scheduled start, and the worktable was already filled with nice handbuilt forms. They looked pretty good, especially considering that these pieces were made by the students and that they had been finished in less than two hours.

Sally demonstrated a fast, simple and straightforward technique that I had never seen before. She started by using a shaped piece of plywood as a template for the base, then laid a slab of clay on it and quickly started building up the form with thick coils. As the form grew, the interior was packed with crushed newspaper to support the form when the top was closed. (The newspaper would burn out during the bisque stage.) The newspaper stuffing allowed the form to fight the force of gravity,

thus speeding up the construction process.

Impressed by Sally's demonstration, I returned to my studio and played around with her technique, making a few simple forms. I sat back and reflected, experimented with a few more, then started to feel there might be something there. I liked whatever was happening, but technical problems began to surface, and I found that I had to learn how to handbuild all over again. Working asymmetrically for the first time, with various parts jutting upward and outward, posed major problems. I didn't have to contend with multiple gravitational pulls as in throwing, but I was trying to work too wet, which caused cracking and sagging problems. While technical problems could always be worked through,

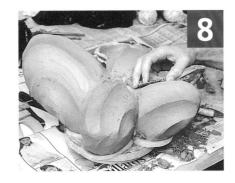

the most important thing was that I was handbuilding and working in a completely new way. This generated a renewed sense of creative vigor in my work and afforded me an opportunity to move on to a new level.

## Process

Place a slab of clay on a wooden board. For this example, I used a piece of plywood for the base, which I had cut in a cloverleaf shape with a jigsaw (figure 1). Place thick coils on the slab and work upward (figure 2). Shape the form as the walls gain height (figure 3). Close off the form one side at a time (figure 4). If needed, crumpled newspaper provides support for wetter clay. Two sides finished (figure 5). I have stopped using the newspaper for this process, relying more on the clay to stiffen as

I work. The basic form is completed and scraped smooth with a serrated rib (figure 6).

## Carving and finishing

If you want to achieve a deeply-carved, more dramatic form, begin with thick walls, then use a rubber rib to recess areas while the clay is relatively soft (figure 7). I use a curved, broken Surform blade to carve and shave the form (figure 8). After rough cutting the form with the Surform tool, I use a metal rib to scrape the form smooth and to clean up the details (figure 9).

The basic form is now completed, awaiting the various parts that will transform it into a teapot (figure 10). Pull the spout as you would pull a handle. Bend it immediately to the shape desired and allow it to dry to

**Finished pieces awaiting the bisque firing.**

a soft leather-hard state. Split it in half like a banana, carve out each half, then reattach with slip. The handle was formed by taking a metal coat hanger and bending it to the desired cross section—essentially a decorative loop tool. Pull the shaped loop through a long, soft block of clay to create the handle (figure 11). Drill a hole for the lid and form a lid. Attach the handle and spout, and the teapot is complete (figure 12).

Copper red carved teapot, 14 inches in length, stoneware,
fired to cone 10 and sandblasted.

Copper red carved form, 14 inches in length, stoneware,
fired to cone 10 and sandblasted.

# Making Large Sculptures with Small Kilns

*by Norma Yuskos*

**"Ruby Lantern,"
27 inches in height,
fired to cone 04,
by Cheryl Tall**

How can a 100-pound woman move, fire, package and ship a 6-foot-tall, 300-pound sculpture all by herself? This was the problem Cheryl Tall faced when she finished graduate school. While working on her M.F.A. at the University of Miami, Florida, huge kilns were available and other people were always around to help with the heavy lifting. However, after graduation, she worked alone in her studio and only had a medium-sized kiln.

As trite as it may seem, Cheryl found that necessity was indeed the mother of invention. She experimented with various sculptural techniques until the result was deceptively simple—sculpture constructions in modules. To give her work stability, she builds internal connections so that each piece is form-fitted into the previous one.

The advantages of her construction method are many. First, each module is fairly easy to lift. While Cheryl could not budge a 300-pound sculpture, she can easily put a 20-pound section into the kiln. Second, Cheryl doesn't need a large kiln,

even for her 6-foot pieces, since the sculpture can be fired in sections. Third, shipping is convenient. It is much simpler to ship several lightweight boxes rather than one huge, heavy crate.

## Forming

The first step in the forming process is to join a few coils to make the outline of the sculpture's base (figure 1).

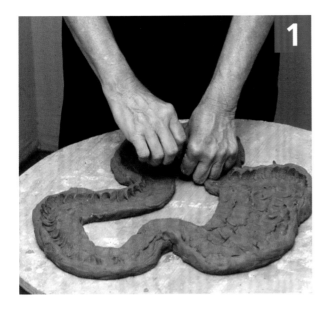

Cheryl uses a cone 04 sculture body with 30% grog. Each coil is about 12 inches long and 1½–2 inches thick. She uses a heavily grogged clay that can take the stress of being worked into a large structure. She adds more coils to the inside, spiraling them around and flattening them to form the base. She leaves a hole, 4–6 inches wide, in the center of the base, which allows air to circulate during drying and firing.

The second step is to build the outer walls. Working with very soft clay, the coils are successfully joined without scoring or using slip. "I use my left thumb and forefinger like a crab claw, pinching the inside and outside at the same time (figure 2). I simultaneously press the clay slightly to join the coil to the previous layer. The right hand guides the coil and keeps the loose end out of the way." This process can be reversed if you are right-handed.

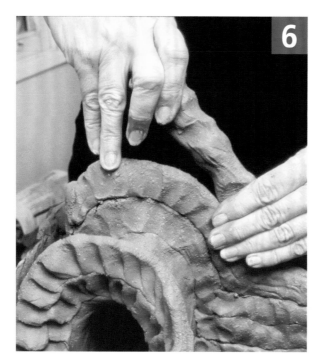

According to Cheryl, "I typically build 10–12 inches at one sitting, but I usually have more than one sculpture in progress at any given time. That way, while a module on one piece is drying, I can work on another." She avoids a smooth surface by accentuating the rhythmic pinching of the clay. In the same way corrugation adds strength to cardboard, the rhythmic pinching adds strength to wet clay. "The corrugated texture may be altered or smoothed during the leather-hard stage by ribbing or

scraping; however, if done during the initial soft-clay stage, the walls will become thin and wobbly. It is also during the leather-hard stage that I add decorative elements such as sprigs, and cutout doors and windows," she explains.

Cheryl developed a system of cone- and platform-shaped connectors inside the sculpture. Around 10–12 inches tall, the sculpture usually becomes unstable. At this point, an inner platform is built, which acts as a stabilizer (figure 3). "Platforms are built of flat sections of clay, ap-

proximately 3 by 6 inches in size and about the same thickness as the walls. I trim these pieces to fit the top edge of the inner wall, and attach them using cross-hatching and slip for extra strength. Each sectional piece should be no wider than 3 inches. As the first section firms up, I add additional pieces side by side in a quilt-like fashion, until the whole platform is built. I place narrow coils at the junction between the platform and the inner edge of the sculpture, and another set of narrow coils on the top of the joints between

10

For the next section, a slab of clay is rolled out slightly larger than the top of the previous section. A hole is cut in the slab and it is placed on top of the paper barrier, with the cone of the previous module protruding through the hole in the center (figure 9). The edges of the slab are trimmed, so they are flush with the wall of the previous module. Then she starts adding coils, repeating the process until the module is complete (figure 10). The modular method is extremely flexible and accommodates the rich detail Cheryl likes to include in her sculptures.

The cone/platform structure gives strength to the walls, provides stability and insures a precise, secure fit between modules. Cheryl explains, "All of the individual sections are separated by paper but are built on top of each other. That way I see the sculpture as a unit, not individual sections." The finished sculpture is air dried, fully assembled, for at least two weeks. Cheryl takes it apart, removes the paper barriers, sands and trims rough spots, and reassembles the work for glazing.

## Glazing

Cheryl prefers to fire her work once. Because the work is not bisqued and is extremely fragile, while glazing, she works slowly and meticulously using a multilayer process that adds depth and definition to each sculpture.

The first step, usually, is to highlight the texture with copper wash. With the sculpture bone dry and ful-

the platform sections. There should be a large 3–4-inch hole remaining in the middle. Cheryl now fiinalizes the module by adding a cone to the platform (figures 4 thru 7) and usually lets the first module firm up before starting the next one.

Before starting the second section, a paper barrier is made to keep the two modules from sticking together (figure 8). Cheryl uses paper towels or newspaper and cuts a hole in the center about the same size as the base of the cone. The barrier is then placed on the platform.

ly assembled, a watercolor brush is used to apply the copper wash to the crevices. A damp sponge is used to remove most of the copper, leaving only an accent.

Next, coats of terra sigillata, slip and commercial underglazes are carefully layered. Cheryl prefers to use these slightly thinned, because if too thick, they tend to crack or peel. For additional dimension, she sometimes gently burnishes the terra sigillata, and uses her own textural glazes and commercial clear glazes for emphasis. Gently spattering clear glaze onto a sculpture with a fan brush gives it a little sparkle without becoming too shiny.

According to Cheryl, "While glazing, I often stand about 10 feet back from the sculpture and look at it though squinted eyes. This helps me to know which areas to accentuate, to lighten, to darken and to change. I try to modulate the colors so that there is a flow from top to bottom."

## Firing

After painting/glazing, the sculpture is assembled in the kiln as far as the height of the kiln will allow. The remaining sections of the sculpture are stacked to the side or fired in another firing.

Since the sculptures have air dried for as much as four weeks and are bone dry, they are fired in an electric kiln on medium or slow ramp without candling. Cheryl usually fires to cone 04 and each firing generally takes 8–12 hours.

## Terra Sigillata

Cone 010–2

This basic formula came from Judy Moonelis. Over time, Cheryl has experimented with various techniques and colorants, and this is what works best for her:

- 12 cups water
- 1000 gm EPK Kaolin
- 500 gm OM4 Kentucky Ball Clay
- 7.5 gm TSP (Trisodium Phosphate) found in hardware stores

Mix the water and TSP. Sift in the EPK and the OM4 and let it slake. Stir and transfer to a clear, covered container. Let it sit undisturbed for 48 hours. DO NOT STIR! The mixture will separate into three layers—water, terra sigillata and sludge (top, middle and bottom, respectively).

### Decanting Methods

POURING—Carefully pour off and discard the clear water at the top. Try not to mix any of the three layers. Pour the next layer, the terra sigillata, into clean 8- or 12-ounce jars with lids. Leave 2 inches of space at the top for adding colorants. The sludge on the bottom of the original container can be discarded, but do not pour it down the sink.

SYPHONING—Cheryl prefers to use a 4–6-foot tube to siphon off the terra sigillata (the middle layer) and discards the remaining two layers.

### Adding Color

The terra sigillata is white. It can be used as is and will take a nice burnish, if desired. Terra sigillata can also be made from colored clays such as Redart by substituting that for the EPK. To make the following colors, add:

**Moldy Bread**—3 tablespoons copper carbonate to ½ cup terra sigillata.

**Sky Blue**—1 tablespoon cobalt carbonate to $1/16$ cup terra sigillata.

**Terra Cotta**—1 tablespoon red iron oxide to $1/8$ cup terra sigillata.

**Sunburn Pink**—1 tablespoon Mason stain 6020 to $1/8$–¼ cup terra sigillata. Add 2 tablespoons of Gerstley borate.

**Tuscany Ochre**—3 tablespoons milled rutile to $1/8$ cup terra sigillata. Add 2 tablespoons of Gerstley borate.

**Apricot**—2 tablespoons Mason stain 6129 to $1/8$–¼ cup terra sigillata. Add 2 tablespoons of Gerstley borate.

After firing, the sculpture is assembled and evaluated. If changes are needed, she will enhance it by adding more slips and glazes, and re-fire the piece. "Room temperature glazes" are sometimes used to add final touches. Cheryl uses fired clay shards to support the bottom of the pieces. These shards will slide on the kiln shelf as the pieces shrink and move during firing. Candling and firing schedules should be developed based on weather and location. Humid conditions, for example, might require longer drying times and/or preheating the kiln at a low temperature to drive away the moisture.

## Room Temperature Glazes

The surface can be enhanced after firing with the following; however, it cannot be re-fired without losing the effects of these new materials.

- Thinned acrylic paints
- Gold leaf or Rub and Buff
- Encaustic paints
- Clear fixative spray
- Minwax, shoe polish, butcher's wax or bowling alley wax
- Oil paints

# Recipes

## Copper Wash

$1/8$ cup Copper Carbonate to 1 cup water. The mix should be the consistency of India ink. More water or copper can be added to get the right consistency. Copper Oxide also can be used. In some cases, Cheryl will use a half and half mixture of Copper Carbonate and Copper Oxide to give it more of a black color in the pre-fired state rather than the verdigris color it usually has.

## Baby Tears
### Cone 04

| | |
|---|---|
| Ferro Frit 3124 . . . . . . . . . . . . . . | 76 % |
| Talc . . . . . . . . . . . . . . . . . . . . | 12 |
| Ball clay . . . . . . . . . . . . . . . . . | 12 |
| | 100 % |

This glaze has a milky, trans-lucent, satin finish.

## Bumby Beads
### Cone 04

| | |
|---|---|
| Magnesium Carbonate . . . . . . . . | 33 % |
| Borax . . . . . . . . . . . . . . . . . . . | 27 |
| Gerstley Borate . . . . . . . . . . . . . | 33 |
| Silica . . . . . . . . . . . . . . . . . . . . | 7 |
| | 100 % |
| Add: Zircopax . . . . . . . . . . . . . . | 7 % |

This glaze provides a pearly, beaded texture and needs to be applied thick.

## Yellow Paint
### Cone 04

| | |
|---|---|
| Gerstley Borate . . . . . . . . . . . . . | 80 % |
| Titanium Dioxide . . . . . . . . . . . . | 20 |
| | 100 % |

This glaze has a creamy, satin finish the color of ochre.

# Handbuilding with Slabs, Cones and Cylinders

*by Scott Dooley*

**"Teapot," 16 inches in height, handbuilt and textured porcelain, fired to cone 5 in a neutral atmosphere.**

Several years ago, when I began handbuilding with slabs, I broke with my previous work, which had been entirely wheel thrown. I started to use plastic pipes and other objects as templates to wrap clay around. At the same time I began handbuilding, I discovered an interest in metal objects, such as funnels, oil cans, mufflers, petroleum storage tanks and grain silos. The overlapping of metal seams, the use of rivets and the aged, weathered look of these forms influenced the direction of my clay work. I began to mimic these metal elements as I developed new forms, cutting and altering the clay to add animation. Through this experimentation, I began to texture and layer oxides and glazes to simulate an aged, weathered surface.

I've primarily produced functional pieces in this new style, relying on the ewer, bottle and teapot forms as the basis for my creations. Working with the teapot and its inherent possibilities is especially enjoyable, and combining parts, like pieces of metal, allows endless combinations.

With this method of building, I have opened up a world of possibilities for creating objects that are distinctly different in process and feel from my previous wheel-thrown work.

## Process

I begin the building process by making the individual parts that will be used in constructing a piece. After rolling out slabs, I cut them to the necessary dimensions. Shown here are the slabs for the body, spout and handle of a teapot. Virtually every part for my work is based on cone and cylinder shapes, which are then

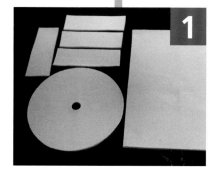

altered (figure 1). To form a spout, I cut a wedge shape out of the circular slab. After the slab has set up, it is formed into a cone, scored on the edges and joined (figure 2). I make a variety of widths for these cones to allow for more options when I am making the spout (figure 3). The handle and body are made by wrapping the slabs around various sizes of PVC pipe. I use newspaper sheaths so the clay will not stick to the plastic. Make sure that the newspaper is not too tight around the pipe; it should easily slide on and off. I overlap the clay about ¼ inch to allow for scoring and joining. Once the clay is joined and stiff enough to hold its own weight, I remove the pipe and newspaper. I then bow the large cylinder into an oval. The parts are left to stiffen a bit more if necessary. Figure 3 shows the beginning parts for

a teapot with the PVC pipes used in the making of the handle and body.

Once the large cylinder is leather hard, I turn it upside down and, using a sharp fettling knife, cut out half circles for the foot (figure 4). I then fit a slab to the bottom, which I score and join. When joining the bottom, take care to cut the slabs to fit together with 45° angles. This allows for a stronger joint, as there is more surface area of the clay joined.

With the bottom slab in place, I turn the cylinder right side up and make the first angled cut into the body (figure 5). It is important that the clay is fairly stiff at this point, or the fettling knife will not make a clean cut. I then turn the top section upside down and make the second cut going the opposite direction on the cylinder, creating a wedge-shaped scrap (figure 6).

The body is then trimmed and sized to fit back to the bottom. This stage takes some patience, but it is very important to have a good tight fit without gaps. I use a sharp scalpel for the small detail trimming when fitting the parts together. Once the pieces are trimmed well, I score and attach the parts (figure 7). Often I need to lean the body up against something to keep it from tipping backwards. I then take small coils of clay and work the seam both on the inside and outside. The next cut is back in the other direction to help balance the body. The process of cutting and attaching is repeated (figure 8). I leave a gap at the back of the body. This allows me to have more freedom in choosing how the last section will attach to the body.

The opening at the back is sealed, using cut and joined slabs. The cre-

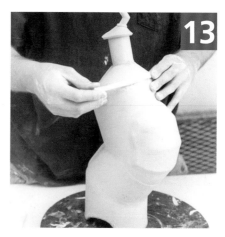

ation of this bulge adds volume to the teapot and gives me a point of connection for the handle (figure 9). The top of the body is a shallow cone shape, and as with the foot, it is joined with 45° angle edges (figure 10).

The lid and neck are added next. The lid is also formed from a shallow cone.

A cylindrical flange is sized to fit inside the neck and then attached to the lid. As a finishing touch, I add a small cylinder to the top of the lid to mimic the body of the teapot (figure 11). At this point, with a metal

ruler, I cut narrow strips of clay from a slab (figure 12). These are added to the attachment points of the foot, top and neck of the teapot (figure 13). They are used to create the look of metal seams.

I begin working on the spout by attaching the largest of the cones to the body. Small coils of clay are used to seal the seam where the spout attaches to the body. I then cut the cone at an angle (figure 14). The next smallest cone is chosen and cut at an angle to fit. It is scored, slipped and attached. Again, small coils are used to smooth the joint. The process is

repeated, altering the angle of the cones (figure 15). When the spout is finished, I add another narrow strip where the spout and body attach. Once the spout is finished, I start the same process with the handle (figure 16). However, I have found that it is easier to attach the handle after the pot is completely assembled. This allows me more freedom to play with the angle of attachment (figure 17).

When the handle is constructed, I texture the whole teapot (figure 18), except for the strips. The possibilities for texturing tools are endless. Most often, my choice is a scrap of concrete. After texturing, I attach the handle and add small strips of clay where the handle joins the body. The final touch is to add small scraps of slabs in various places on the teapot. These will remain untextured and will be glazed a different color than the body of the teapot (figure 19).

## Glazing

Once the teapot has been bisque fired, I apply a layer of black copper oxide mixed with water. This is then sponged off, leaving oxide in the textured areas. The clay strips have a thicker layer of oxide applied to them. This layer is lightly sponged to keep it from being too thick. I then spray glaze over the oxide. The oxide will burn through the glaze and remain black. Black copper oxide will run if it is on too thick. One needs to experiment with it in combination with one's glazes before trying it on a finished piece. I texture my test tiles on one side so I can see the result of the oxide on a glaze both with and without texture.

**"Industrial Bottles,"** to 23 inches in height, handbuilt and textured porcelain, fired to cone 5. The texture on the bottles was achieved by pressing found metal objects into the surface of the clay before it was formed into cylinders and cones.

**"Two Ewers,"** 7 inches in height, handbuilt and textured porcelain, gas fired to cone 5 in a neutral atmosphere.

## Joining Slips

The joining slip I make works very well for handbuilding. I have used several different clay bodies with this building method, and the slip has held up. The Darvan 7 deflocculant allows one to use less water in the slip. This, in turn, means that there will be less shrinkage at the joints where it is used. The powdered clay is prepared from leftover scraps that have dried out. Currently, I am using a commercial porcelain body.

First, I mix the Darvan 7 and water together in a pint container. I then add powdered clay, mixing until I get the desired consistency. It is easier to add dry clay, as it absorbs into the solution more quickly. I like the slip to be thick enough to brush on. It is best to let the slip sit for a day or so, to avoid chunks in the mixture.

### Dooley's Joining Slip

Approx. 2 tsp. of Darvan 7 deflocculant
½ pint water
Dry, powdered clay body

"Industrial Stirrup Bottle," 22 inches in height, handbuilt and textured porcelain, fired to cone 5 in a neutral atmosphere.

"Teapot, Creamer and Sugar," to 12 inches in height, handbuilt and textured porcelain, fired to cone 5 in a neutral atmosphere.

# Dong Hee Suh
## A Slice of Paradise

*by Glen R. Brown*

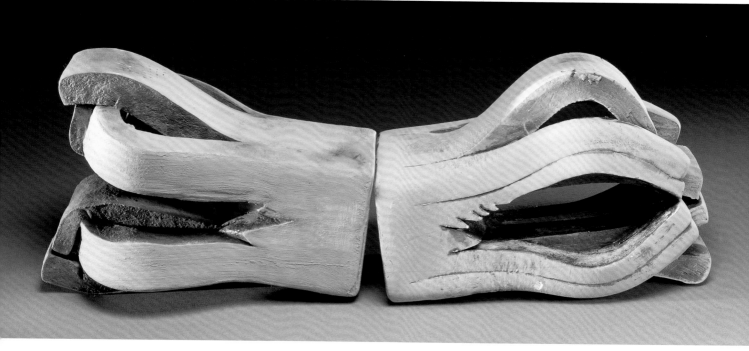

**"River 1," 15 inches in length, sliced stoneware, fired to cone 04.**

Curiously, the Biblical Garden of Eden has only rarely been the subject of representation in the history of art, even during those many centuries when the church exercised unyielding influence over the content of European painting and sculpture. Moreover, those images in which Eden has appeared have tended to be relatively mundane. Hieronymus Bosch's "Paradise" seems sedate, almost dull in comparison with the tumultuous (and sinful) festivity of his "Garden of Earthly Delights" and the terrors of his weirdly imaginative Hell. The most famous representation of Eden, Michelangelo's Sistine "Temptation and Expulsion,"

is surprisingly reserved, even bland, in contrast to the artist's powerful depiction of damnation in the "Last Judgement."

Why this distinction should have occurred in Michelangelo's work is an interesting point of speculation. Perhaps fear proved a greater stimulus to his imagination than desire; perhaps one who would later humble himself by rendering a self portrait in the flayed skin of St. Bartholomew was naturally reluctant to assume the arrogance implicit in the claim to a clear vision of Paradise; or perhaps Michelangelo, and many of those countless others who never attempted to represent the most perfect of earthly landscapes, believed

"The Tree of Knowledge," 12 inches in height, sliced stoneware, fired to cone 04.

that the Garden of Eden possessed more power as an elusive ideal than it could ever generate as a concrete image.

In a series entitled "The Garden of Eden," Korean ceramist Dong Hee Suh reflects a similar reluctance to treat her theme with the specificity of firsthand observation, choosing instead merely to hint at the perfection of Eden through highly abstract forms. The titles of individual works suggest that Suh has not forsaken representation for pure nonobjectivity, but her forms nonetheless seem more attuned to an autonomous lyricism than to the illustration of specific objects. She is, in fact, concerned with conveying through her sculptures an otherwise inexpressible feeling about Eden, a place that touches her intuition but that cannot be clearly envisioned. Her goal is to communicate to the viewer a conviction about paradise that is founded on faith rather than confirmed through experience.

To speak of faith in connection with artistic inspiration today—even faith in something as simple as the ability of art to embody specific meanings—is to court controversy. Faith is a condition of belief in the absence of evidence, and as such has found itself in a bind between the demands for verification made by empiricists and the claims to relativity made by contemporary theorists of language and representation. Faith scandalizes the former by accepting the truthfulness of intangibles and it antagonizes the latter by insisting that the veracity of its objects is not arbitrary but real. Faith grapples for something that is perceived as simultaneously certain and as unverifiable, even untestable. It has always come down to feeling rather than logic. Understanding this, Suh filled her garden with forms that are not self-evident as representations, but which convey obvious emotion.

Suh's slicing technique, which involves the emergence of complex form from a larger previously undifferentiated whole, could be compared to the method used by the Abstract Expressionist painter Barnett Newman to create his famous "zip" compositions. On a monochrome canvas, Newman affixed a vertically oriented strip of masking tape, then repainted the exposed surface in a different tone or hue. Removing the tape revealed a crisp band, the result of an action

that the artist compared to the account of creation in Genesis: through separation, the one undifferentiated being acquires many modes of being, among them humanity. For Suh, the act of slicing in such a way that a mass acquires parts but remains a single being is a perfect metaphor for the Biblical creation. In her Garden of Eden, form, content and technique are thus integrally connected to one another.

A professor of ceramics at Konkuk University (KU) in Seoul, Korea, Suh developed her unusual technique of working clay while she was a graduate student at the University of Kansas. Having previously studied ceramics at Seoul National University, where the focus was exclusively on vessel making, she was intrigued by the strong emphasis on ceramic sculpture in the United States. Her lack of experience with sculpting techniques actually proved to be an asset when she began experimenting with nonfunctional objects in clay. Uninhibited by a conventional knowledge of modeling, carving and assemblage, she simply applied a basic tool in a way that made sense to her. Ever since, slicing has been her central technique, acquiring a strong metaphorical dimension as her work has developed.

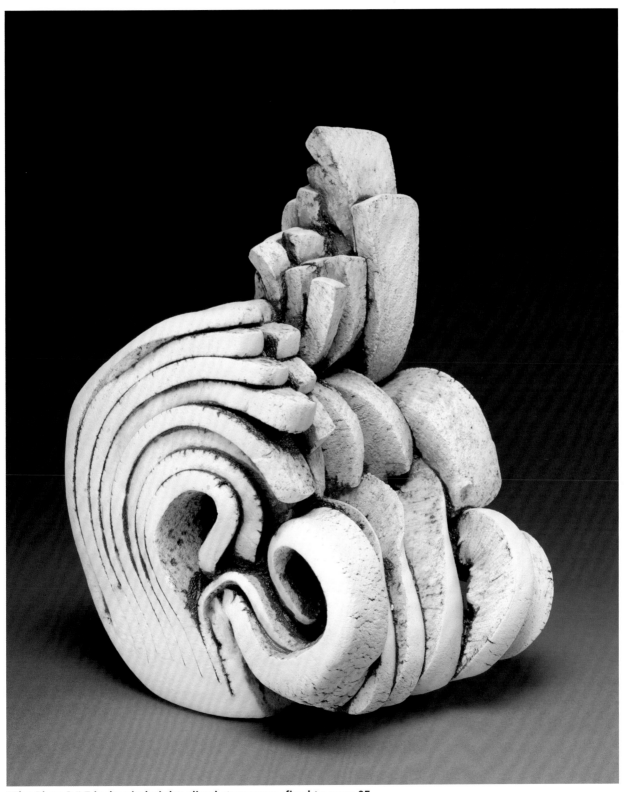

"The River 3," 7 inches in height, sliced stoneware, fired to cone 05.

## Sculpting with Wire

Suh's unusual manner of sculpting is well suited to allusions to energy or spirit. Described by Richard Zakin in his Hand-Formed Ceramics: Creating Form and Surfaces as virtually unique among the techniques of contemporary ceramists, her method involves not carving, modeling or assemblage, but slicing: an action that Suh has compared to cutting a loaf of bread. Starting with a rectangular or other geometrically shaped block of wet clay, she makes a series of vertical slices with a wire, sometimes removing sections of clay and sometimes merely separating the clay into thin slabs or fingerlike divisions. These are then gently bowed into drooping and unfurling clusters that resemble plant forms. Sparse application of low-fire glazes to the finished pieces heightens their impression of botanical delicacy.

"Wavy 2," 8½ inches in height, sliced stoneware, fired to cone 1, by Dong Hee Suh, Seoul, Korea.

It has always been on the level of the abstract that Suh feels most at home. She has long valued art primarily as a vehicle for expressing inner, otherwise private, experience rather than as a means of duplicating external forms. As a consequence, she is not obsessive about precise communication but rather is content with conveying a general feeling, a sense of spirit and energy that is formed within the sphere of the personal but which possesses the potential to touch another's sensibility as well. Although her work has drawn inspiration from Biblical texts, she does not wish to illustrate specific stories, nor is she particularly concerned about whether or not her viewers pay attention to the representational aspect of her work. Some respond to her forms only on a general aesthetic level, and Suh does not demand anything more.

Her Garden of Eden could thus be seen as a moving array of emotive forms in which potential exists to raise intuitive spiritual responses in the viewer: a parallel to the modern images of artists such as Wassily Kandinsky, Alexei von Jawlensky, Barnett Newman or Mark Rothko. In her garden, Suh cultivates more than the narrow, representational potential of form. She is confident of the veracity of her content, but equally convinced of the futility of imposing it upon the viewer. As a reference to paradise, a compelling but elusive ideal carried deeply within the mind, Suh's Garden of Eden could not adopt more persuasive means.

# Making Large Jars

*by Karen Terpstra*

I came rather late to ceramics and my work focused on handbuilding with painterly images of the horse. As my process involved wood firing, I found the need for larger surface areas that would hold an image and be integrated with the flash and ash from the wood-fire process. Handbuilt jars that defy gravity in their form fulfill that need. Horse images with a spontaneous degree of abstraction have gradually developed from mental impressions of historical myths—others are in response to real horses I have known.

Making large jars with flat coils has been done for centuries in many parts of Asia and Southeast Asia. Master potters in Korea made thousands of flat-coiled storage jars—primarily used for kimchi, the national dish of Korea, which is comprised of pickled vegetables seasoned with garlic, red pepper and ginger. Once the basic method is learned, anyone can make large jars (or any size functional or sculptural object) with a flat coil method. I started learning with small jars and teapots, but now I make large jars that defy gravity and would normally collapse if wheel thrown. I also make many sculptural forms—horse heads, large full-body horses, torsos and columns—using this method.

As you can see from the photographs, one big advantage with this method is that you can change directions rather drastically by letting the flat coils become leather hard. Another advantage is the variety of sculptural forms you can make. This method also saves a lot of time by using 2-inch flat coils instead of small round coils.

It's really time saving to work in a series. Build up three to six rows of "coils" on several ware boards at one time. By the time you're finished with the last one, you can start again on the first one.

## Process

Roll the clay through the slab roller about ⅛ to ¼ inch larger than your desired wall thickness. The walls

Wood-fired, hand-built jars by Karen Terpstra. She states, "I try not to predetermine too much of the form when I start but rather let the hand-building process determine the ultimate result. I am primarily concerned with the structure of the form, and how the shape, drawings and surface relate."

PROCESS PHOTOGRAPHS BY DON ANDERSON.

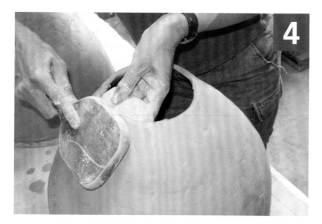

will be thinner by the time you smooth and paddle the shape. Cut the clay into flat coils about 2 inches wide for a large jar (figure 1).

Slightly dampen the ware board or bat with a sponge for the first flat coil. Attach the flat coil firmly in place then secure another flat coil. Since you will be building the lower section of the jar upside down, place the flat coil to the inside of the previous flat coil. This makes the diameter become smaller with each row (figure 2). Also, put plastic on the inside of the jar to hold in the moisture. Smooth the seams inside and out while building (figure 3). Let the first few rows strengthen to

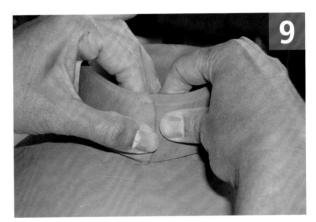

leather hard so that they will hold the weight of additional coils. Once the lower portion is leather hard, keep it wrapped in plastic, so that it doesn't dry out as you continue to work. Once the lower portion of the jar is completed and leather hard, you need to strengthen the walls. I use a paddle and a rounded piece of wood I call an "anvil," which I hold on the inside of the pot (figure 4). This technique also helps to obtain the desired shape.

Cut out a circle from a slab for the bottom of the jar. Slip, score and attach the bottom (figure 5). Paddle it to reinforce the seam (figure 6).

Cover the piece and let it strengthen overnight. This also allows the moisture content to equalize.

The next morning, turn the jar over, and score and slip the edge. Since the form will be very leather hard by this time, add a small round coil to the edge (figure 7). The fresh coil provides an anchor to work off of while adding more flat coils. Now that the jar is right side up, you can add the shoulder (figure 8). Cut out a rim from a slab and attach to the top of the jar. Sometimes I smooth the jar a bit more, or alter the rim by rotating it slowly on the wheel and using a wet sponge or rib (figure 9).

Wood-fired, handbuilt jars by Karen Terpstra. She states, "I try not to predetermine too much of the form when I start but rather let the hand-building process determine the ultimate result. I am primarily concerned with the structure of the form, and how the shape, drawings and surface relate."

I've always been interested in horses, probably from owning and raising several of them since early childhood. This interest is directed to finding form in my imagery of them, specifically in sculpture and ceramics.

# Nancy Jurs
## Turning to Ancient Wisdom

*by Shirley M. Dawson*

**"Full Circle," 72 inches in height with base, from the "Armor" series, stoneware with copper patina.**

Nancy Jurs strides toward the door to answer my knock. I see her approaching through the front door windows and realize how imperceptibly she has changed over the years. She moves with the self confidence of an athlete, an assurance that muscles will respond predictably to demands. Nearly every day for forty years, she has managed the heft of wet clay. It is a physically demanding career.

Before the interview begins, Jurs gives me a tour of her 100-year-old farmhouse. Art projects in various stages of completion are scattered throughout the house. In one room, there is a chorus of dressmaker mannequins and a collection of antique shoetrees. In another room, carefully saved stacks of dryer lint are all sculpture-ready raw material.

Jurs becomes slightly defiant describing this work, a revealing glimpse of a woman demanding to be taken seriously as an artist. It is a common posture understood and often shared by anyone whose life work is made in a clay studio. "Clay has never had the credit it is due.

After all, the material has no intrinsic beauty—not like glass or wood or even metal." She is right. The love of the material comes from its malleability, the sensuousness of touch.

Just down the road from her home is the tiny village of Scottsville, New York. Quiet streets are lined with ancient maple trees and charming but modest 19th-century houses. Two minutes from Main Street, in what was once a Victorian train station, is Jurs' ceramics studio.

If Jurs' attention seemed scattered at home, she is entirely focused here. There is a high-pitched hum of activity the day I visit. Three assistants are committed to whatever tasks she has laid out for them in preparation for a solo exhibition and several group commitments. Shipping trucks are nearly here and if Jurs experiences job-related stress, it is not visible. She seems totally in charge of the scene.

"Triad," 16 feet in height, handbuilt stoneware, fired in an industrial kiln, and installed at the Greater Rochester International Airport, Rochester, New York.

On our way to the back of the studio to see the newest large sculpture pieces, we pass shelves loaded with wheel-thrown pots—bowls with slightly asymmetrical shapes, glazes deftly applied. They sell in museum and gallery shops around the country at affordable prices, providing the base income for the studio.

Jurs' career in clay began when she entered the School of American Crafts at Rochester Institute of Technology (RIT). She was seventeen years old, fresh out of high school with no clue about her future. Her mother's cousin, LuLu Scott Backus, was a pioneer clay educator at RIT during the 1920s. Another cousin, Eunice Prieto, studied at Alfred University and later taught ceramics at Mills College in California. Not many women were looking to clay as a career in the 1960s, but not many had these family prototypes to guide them!

Frans Wildenhain and Hobart Cowles headed the RIT ceramics department during those years. Clay was mostly about chemistry and technical skill. It was quickly obvious that Jurs had talent and a natural aptitude for clay.

Changes in ceramics aesthetics, as well as technical advances, came at breathtaking speed during the '60s and '70s. Jurs' work changed with the times. She experimented with clay bodies, construction and firing techniques. A personal style and color palette began to emerge.

Jurs spent an apprenticeship wheel throwing and marketing functional dinnerware and mugs; however, early in her career, her handbuilt pots took on the pendulous, voluptuous shapes of body parts with near-sexy surfaces and colors to match. They straddled the line between function and sculpture. Later, these vessels gave way to nearly pure-white, too-precious, little-girl blouses. They stood on tabletops, sized for toddler baby dolls, and, at the time, seemed a step backward in Jurs' art evolution. Actually, they provided clues to her next serious body of work.

In the '80s, Jurs created a series of raku-fired ceramic breastplates. "They were female armor," says Jurs, "but I can't tell you how many people remember them as masculine figures." Gone was the innocence of the porcelain blouse vases. The first round of this body armor was muscular, metallic, flinty and aggressive, and in tune with the feminine

**Nancy Jurs fitted a bow saw with a wire instead of a blade to shape large torsos for her "Armor" series.**

political climate of the times. These sculptures seemed to open a creative floodgate for Jurs.

During the following years, the breastplates grew to human-scale, floor-standing abstractions that she named "The Goddesses." Constructed and fired in sections from slabs of stoneware, some grew mermaid tails and flower-bulb abdomens. Their surfaces were brushed with expressionistic motifs. The little-girl blouses recurred but this time as tiny busts attached to cactuslike bodies striking sassy poses. Mostly, they were less authoritarian, more playful than earlier breastplates. Aggression was replaced

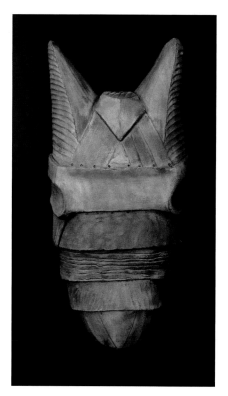

**"Ahead of Time,"** wall piece 34 inches in height, stoneware with copper patina, fired to cone 5, by Nancy Jurs, Scottsville, New York.

with wit. Whether pretty or prickly, her work clearly had something to say beyond clay process and aesthetics. Jurs used art to talk about ideas: women and girls, their roles, social and self-imposed constraints.

Jurs won a design commission to create an installation in a rotunda at the newly built Monroe County (New York) International Airport. She built "Triad"; three solid figures carved out of 12,000 pounds of clay. They stand on bowed monster legs 15 feet high and required her to invent a unique new construction technique, enlarge her studio to accommodate the eighteen sections and collabo-

rate with an industrial facility that had kilns large enough to fire these giants. Triad remains an awesome achievement—one of the largest sculptures, Jurs believes, installed by a modern clay artist. Certainly, it catapulted Jurs into a new art arena. She has since completed several other major public art pieces—dwarfs by comparison, standing 6 to 8 feet tall—and launched a series of free-standing sculpture she calls "The Rock Series."

September 11, 2001. Jurs, like many artists, went to the studio to find a personal way to deal with the plethora of emotions. Jurs says, "my emotions switched to an urgent search for protection."

"Armor Series," a new body of work, was introduced at the Castellani Art Museum in February 2004. The first armor series was called The Goddesses, and this series might be appropriately titled the "Council of Wise Women." The sculptural garments are inspired by historical Asian design. Matt surfaces and pastel copper greens of metal patinas seem nearly like velvet. These clay robes fall into graceful, multilayered folds, and each stands more than 6 feet high on its pedestal. The effect is startling. The sculptures seem to stand in witness of historical events—not so much protecting, but silently marking the sad march of chaos. With this body of work, Jurs has turned to ancient wisdom for comfort—not a bad place to look for inspiration both artistically and politically.

# Challenging Beauty
## The Sculpture of Tom Bartel

*by Anderson Turner*

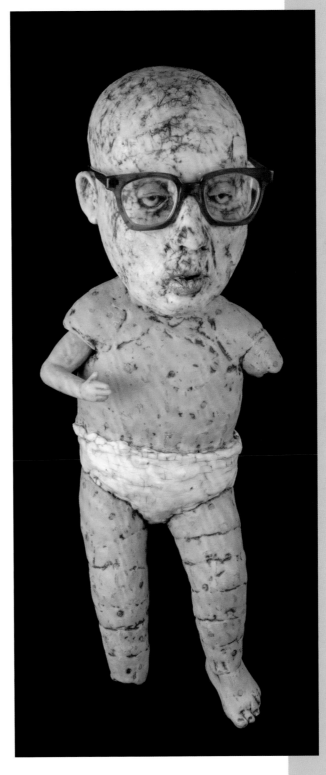

"Figure with Diaper and Glasses," 20 inches in height, hand-built, with vitreous engobes and black copper oxide, fired multiple times.

There is a place in our minds that we all know about, but it's a part of our consciousness that we deny or pay little attention to. On occasion, we find ourselves delving into this part of our head and using what we find as a tool. The work of Tom Bartel touches places of the brain such as this. What exactly it means and what it points to is unresolved, but its expression is unavoidable. The work has a power beyond the artist's hand that connects to and disrupts the viewer's life.

It has been argued that people react more positively to representational art because it leads them down a road that is more comfortable or familiar to them. What happens when that road of comfort becomes twisted, confused and all together abstract? Hopefully, the viewer, while being subverted, will find themselves in an area that is perhaps new and exciting, or at least thought provoking.

"Challenging" is an easy way to describe Bartel's work, which explores and proffers his interpretation of

**Tom Bartel uses basic pinch and coil-building techniques when making his figures.**

plore topics like time, birth, aging, sexuality, beauty and our attitudes toward them. The work is by no means easily digested. The characters Bartel creates are reminiscent of many horror movies made popular by Hollywood and, at the same time, remind viewers of people they know.

The strength of Bartel's work lies in its ability to straddle the line between humor, religious and historical imagery, and the familiar. His sculptures depict vulnerable human forms that are often changed by outside influences.

"My work is consistently being interpreted as disturbing (and humorous) to many viewers," Bartel explains. "This theme is not a conscious pursuit of mine, rather it is simply an outcome that I see over and over . . . and evidently something that is important to me."

In his piece, "Figure with Diaper and Glasses," Bartel and his approach come through clearly. The piece, which is a baby-sized figure in a diaper with an older persons head and Buddy Holly–style glasses, has a doll-like quality. However, unlike a doll it holds an expression that is decidedly human, as if to say, "What the heck happened to me?" There is an arm and foot missing, and the arm that does exist looks as if it has been torn off and put back on poorly. The diaper appears to be almost one with the figure, as if it were knitted on. One could say this doll had a rough day, but this piece is far too human for that, and further inspec-

human beauty. There are many interpretations of the meaning of human beauty. To many, it is the young female model posing on the pages of a fashion magazine. To others, it is the colors of a sunset reflected in the face of the one they've been married to for 40 years. Bartel, while using the human form as representational subject matter, manipulates it to extion will only remind the onlooker of someone injured or disfigured in some way.

"My doll pieces are intended to reference toys, but also to blur the line between doll and human," Bartel states. "Dolls are potent objects. I believe all objects have inherent power, which artists may choose to use or abuse. I enjoy the ambiguity, generalization and confusion sometimes found in my work, as well as the contradictory messages they are capable of sending."

Bartel talks a lot about the "subtle influences of time" when he describes his own aesthetic. It is hard to see anything subtle about the work. What is perhaps most off putting is the use of the doll and the older looking decrepit human form. A person must imagine the life of that doll and all that can happen over a lifetime. Was the doll born like that, or did all of the damage happen in an accident, or over time? Did the doll have children? Is this thing in pain?

While contemplating the meaning of Bartel's art, one must note the importance he places on his choice of material. "I'm not an artist who happens to teach clay. I am an artist who works in clay, and I am very proud of that. . . . One thing I really love about ceramics is that it is so well grounded in the ancient past—our past," he says. "I work intuitively, following the lead of the material. I am merely the conduit between the material and my ideas. I make a lot of work. As a student, I was exposed to the importance of be-

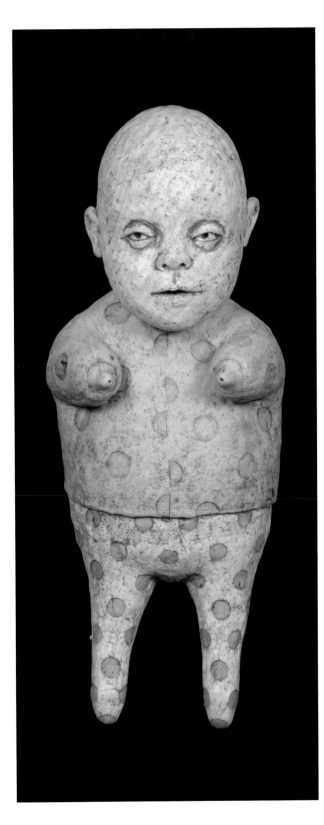

"Fertile Boy,"
20 inches in height, handbuilt, with vitreous engobes, black copper oxide and "Low-Tech" Pink Terra Sigillata, fired multiple times.

Top: "Disconnected Figure," 24 inches in height, handbuilt, with vitreous engobes and black copper oxide, fired multiple times.

Bottom: "Texican Wrestler," 12 inches in height, handbuilt, with vitreous engobes, black copper oxide and red terra sigillata, fired multiple times, by Tom Bartel, Bowling Green, Kentucky.

ing prolific. Really, there is no other way to grow. I see it in my students every semester; the give and take dynamics of the academic studio environment I'm sure also is a factor. Allowing myself to be influenced by everything and anything—being observant and persistent—is important. Our job as visual artists is to 'funnel' everything we find interesting and important, and to 'sieve' that which doesn't help us, no matter the source. Taking risks is important.

"Sometimes, I intend to generalize or even edit parts of the body. Often this is achieved simply by paying attention to the material, and having a sense of economy and sensitivity in the process. What's absent is as important as what's present. Stephen DeStaebler said something to this affect: 'I find that there is a greater sense of wholeness when the whole is not there.' In poetry, it's often the spaces or gaps between the words that are most powerful."

Perhaps that is what is most important about Bartel's work. He leaves questions and wonderment, as opposed to direct answers, in the pieces he makes. Through his exploration of sexual identity, aging, time and because of the vulnerability a little fear can bring, Tom Bartel is making thought-provoking and interesting work.

"Crummy Mummy," 7 inches in height, handbuilt, with vitreous engobes, black copper oxide and white terra sigillata, fired multiple times.

## Low-Tech Construction and Multifiring

*by Tom Bartel*

My techniques are quite simple and low tech. I make coil-built and pinched forms—things we learned in grade school. There are obvious connections between the body and pots, and I manipulate the volume of my figures much like a vessel.

I apply vitreous engobes, terra sigillata and a few glazes to leather-hard clay. The engobe is fired to cone 02. Then black copper or other oxide washes are applied, and the piece is again fired to cone 02. I often fire and refire until the desired effect is achieved or the piece is destroyed. Many unexpected things occur during the firing process that I enjoy being challenged by . . . these things sometimes take my ideas/process to unexpected places.

Bartel often uses low-tech resist material as well; in this case stickers.

# Recipes

## Mangus/Kwong All-Purpose Clay Body

### Cone 04–10

| | |
|---|---|
| Wollastonite | 4.1% |
| Ball Clay | 0.4 |
| Earthenware | 39.8 |
| Fireclay | 39.8 |
| Sand | 15.9 |
| | 100.0% |

## Bronze/Black

### Cone 02

| | |
|---|---|
| Ferro Frit 3110 | 9% |
| Copper Carbonate | 18 |
| Manganese Dioxide | 73 |
| | 100% |

This works best when brushed on very thin, and fired in a gas kiln.

## Tom Bartel's Toad Belly

### Cone 04–02

| | |
|---|---|
| Borax | 19% |
| Gerstley Borate | 37 |
| Magnesium Carbonate | 37 |
| Silica | 7 |
| | 100% |
| Add: Zircopax | 15% |

This off-white glaze is dry, and it cracks. More borax may be needed when fired to cone 04.

## Tom's Crawl

### Cone 04

| | |
|---|---|
| Borax | 3.9% |
| Gerstley Borate | 46.5 |
| Magnesium Carbonate | 31.0 |
| EPK Kaolin | 18.6 |
| | 100.0% |
| Add: Zircopax | 5.4% |

This is a translucent, globby crawling glaze.

## "AC" Dry Matt Glaze

### Cone 04

| | |
|---|---|
| Barium Carbonate | 23.9% |
| Lithium Carbonate | 4.6 |
| Ferro Frit 3110 | 9.1 |
| Nepheline Syenite | 50.5 |
| EPK Kaolin | 5.5 |
| Silica | 6.4 |
| | 100.0% |
| Add: Bentonite | 18.3% |

## Red Pleather Engobe

### Cone 02

| | |
|---|---|
| Gerstley Borate | 20% |
| Redart | 80 |
| | 100% |

## Bartel Engobe Base

### Cone 02

| | |
|---|---|
| Borax | 4.5% |
| Gerstley Borate | 9.1 |
| Ferro Frit 3110 | 31.9 |
| Ball Clay | 13.6 |
| Kaolin | 27.3 |
| Silica | 13.6 |
| | 100.0% |

This base is meant to be colored with commercial stains, not oxides.

## Engobe Base

### Cone 02

| | |
|---|---|
| Borax | 2.4% |
| Gerstley Borate | 4.9 |
| Ferro Frit 3110 | 34.2 |
| Ball clay | 14.6 |
| Kaolin | 29.3 |
| Silica | 14.6 |
| | 100.0% |

This base is formulated for use with oxides, not commercial stains. It has less flux than the Bartel Engobe Base, which prevents overfiring.

## Tom's Skin Glaze #5

### Cone 06–03

| | |
|---|---|
| Gerstley Borate | 37.5% |
| Wollastonite | 62.5 |
| | 100.0% |

When fired to cone 06, this is dry, off-white, and it cracks.

## Tom's Skin Glaze #6

### Cone 06–03

| | |
|---|---|
| Gerstley Borate | 42% |
| Wollastonite | 53 |
| Silica | 5 |
| | 100% |

At cone 04, this has very nice globby cracking texture.

## Tom's Skin Glaze #7

### Cone 06–03

| | |
|---|---|
| Gerstley Borate | 33% |
| Wollastonite | 56 |
| Ball Clay | 11 |
| | 100% |

At cone 04, this is a nice milky translucent glaze. At Cone 06, it becomes too dry.

## Tom's Skin Glaze #8

### Cone 06–03

| | |
|---|---|
| Gerstley Borate | 38% |
| Wollastonite | 48 |
| Ball Clay | 14 |
| | 100% |

At cone 04, this has a nice globby cracking, similar to #6 but with softer edges (brains!).

## "Low-Tech" Pink Terra Sigillata

| | |
|---|---|
| Ball clay | 75% |
| Redart clay | 25 |
| | 100% |

Dry mix the clays and add them to water. Mix in 1 teaspoon of calgon. In a few days, decant the water from the top and save the middle layer, which is the stuff you want.

For white, use ball clay only, or use equal parts ball clay and kaolin. Repeat the above procedure. This also may be used as a base for the addition of other colorants. Test colorants by starting with 1/3 cup of base and adding 1 or 2 teaspoons of colorant.

# Fractals Wrapped in Clay

*by Elina Brandt-Hansen*

Detail of "Spirals," colored porcelain, using a rope technique (thin sheets of porcelain are rolled onto sheets of stoneware, then wrapped around rope, which is then torn out), fired to 2336°F.

E ven our sky is filled with patterns. To our eyes, the constellations do not make any detailed composition, but I like to think that this is because we are too close. If we could watch our sky from farther out in space than any satellite has ever been, then the stars and the solar systems may just be a small part of a pattern-covered fractal stretching to the other side of the universe.

Without knowing anything about fractal geometry, I had been repeating patterns within my work for many years. I didn't learn about fractals until I received a video on them from a person who had seen my work. Seeing that video was magi-cal. It made me eager and curious to explore the endless possibilities that fractal geometry seemed to offer.

A fractal is a geometric pattern that is repeated at an ever smaller scale producing irregular shapes and surfaces that cannot be represented by classical geometry. Fractal geometry implies that every little detail is a reflection of the whole unit, and that the whole unit is reflected in even the smallest detail.

In nature, we can observe fractals in a leaf of a plant or in the florets of a cauliflower. The tiny feather of a bird also consists of thousands of fractals. A single cell from a human body carries within its DNA all the information needed to create an

"Deconstruction," 26 inches square, stoneware and porcelain, formed around wooden dowels, with transparent glaze, bronze luster and red enamel, fired to 2336°F.

"Cross Structure," 22 inches square, stoneware elements wrapped in colored porcelain, assembled into crosses and attached to the surface of a layered stoneware and porcelain form, with transparent glaze, black enamel and gold luster, fired to 2336°F.

exact copy of the body. Every material, whether it is a solid, liquid or gas, consists of an unbelievable complexity of patterns and compositions. I am convinced that patterns and fractals are essential to existence.

Since childhood, patterns and ornaments have fascinated and inspired me. As the years go by, I recognize the changes in the patterns and rhythms of my own development as an artist. When I was about 12 years old, my mother taught me how to create and sew my own clothes. At age 14, I was introduced to clay at an after-school course. After high school, I spent many years at different handicraft schools where I could develop these interests.

Because both fabric and clay had been important to me during my youth, it seemed natural for me to

combine the two materials when I attended the National College of Art and Design in Bergen in 1980. After some years of carrying my half-finished ceramic pieces to different stores in order to find fabric with the right color and texture, my teacher, Ole Lislerud, persuaded me to abandon the fabric. He convinced me that, in order to combine clay and fabric successfully, I would have to know as much about fabric as I did about clay. I realized that I did not want to study four and a half years in the textile department in addition to the time I had already committed to studying ceramics. Clay was the medium through which I could best express myself.

My new challenge became one of transferring my favorite qualities of fabric into clay. In the last six months

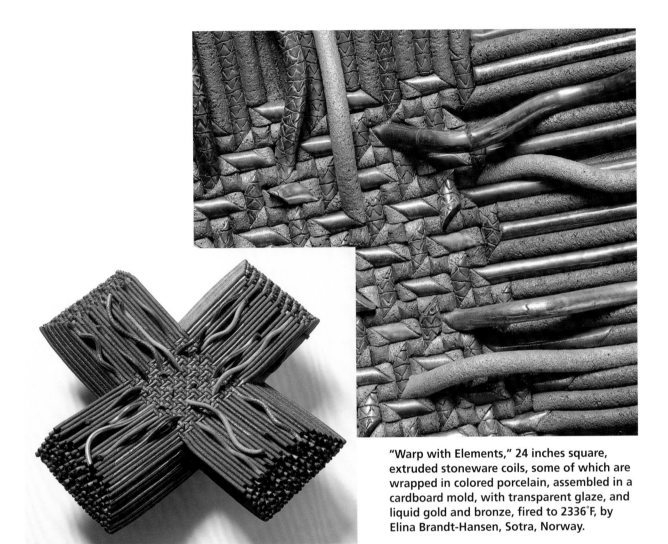

"Warp with Elements," 24 inches square, extruded stoneware coils, some of which are wrapped in colored porcelain, assembled in a cardboard mold, with transparent glaze, and liquid gold and bronze, fired to 2336°F, by Elina Brandt-Hansen, Sotra, Norway.

of college, I assembled thousands of small stoneware pieces, colored in subtle blacks and browns, into vases and other container forms. I felt, however, that the resulting patterns looked more like basketwork than fabric.

After graduating and then taking some time off for the birth of my son, I was offered a job as a scholarship holder in the ceramics department of the National College of Art and Design by my mentor, Arne Åse.

During this time, I researched and experimented with colored stoneware and porcelain.

My husband and I purchased a house in the little village of Klokkarvik and I set up my studio in the basement. I built a concrete building for my 21-cubic-foot electric kiln and started working on my first solo exhibition.

A few weeks after the opening I received two invitations: one to come to the Banff Centre in Canada; and a second to be an artist-in-residence in both Canberra and Hobart in Australia. I was totally overwhelmed because I did not have any specific ambition when setting up my studio, and this was my very first exhibition. My only wish was to express myself in clay, whether it was through ashtrays or door signs for my new neighbors. After this initial contact, early in my career, with great international ceramics artists like Leslie Manning, Alan Watt and Les Blakebrough, the ball just kept rolling.

For ten years, most of my pieces have been based upon detailed sketches. Usually, I do not allow my pieces to differ from the sketch during the working process, because every color, line and angle has been precisely planned for a certain purpose—whether it be an optical illusion, a specific movement, a certain depth or color displacement. Often, when people see these complicated compositions they ask if I am particularly interested in mathematics. To be honest, math was my worst subject at school. Fortunately, this doesn't matter because my work is very logical to me. It is like all the needed information is already there within the piece itself. My challenge is to become aware of all the interesting possibilities of compositions one single element is able to create.

After spending up to four weeks to make hundreds of complicated components for a specific piece, I prefer not to risk wasting them by experimenting. However, I always make more ornaments than needed for the

piece so I can experiment with the leftovers. Every piece becomes the source of new ideas for my future work.

Sometimes, with simple pieces, I am too eager to start assembling the parts and cannot wait until the sketch or the picture of the piece is clear in my head. For example, I might notice a sunbeam shining through my little basement window drawing lovely shadows on the form, and this may inspire a different direction. Such events always seem to happen when I need them to. They provide unexpected, welcome new ideas of how to finish my piece.

I also have become much more aware of what is happening on my table when working. Making a piece always produces lots of scrap clay of different colors and shapes. When tidying my table, I try to have an open eye to all the mess that has piled up. Often I find new ideas or the solution to a problem laying right in front of me.

Eventually, I started to wrap clay around different kinds of rope. This was a natural progression after having worked with coils of clay. When the rope is removed, it leaves a hollow coil of colored clay. I also started to wrap wooden sticks and wooden balls. I was quite pleased to see the emergent structure that this technique produced because I was quite tired of sketching.

At this point, three-dimensional structures and textures are more important than two-dimensional composition. Even though these works

"Swarm," 22 inches in diameter, stoneware-backed colored porcelain is wrapped around rope and attached to a stoneware platter. The platter is then sprinkled with underglaze powder, and the rope is torn out of the clay, exposing the colored-porcelain pattern.

do not require demanding sketches, they are equally time consuming. To create a desired surface effect, I sometimes have to wrap 130 feet of rope with clay. Even though the fractal geometry no longer is as obvious as it once was, it is still present in the way that I choose and arrange the colors. When looking into certain details of a piece, one can discover a multicolored porcelain pattern that includes all the colors used throughout the whole structure.

By building up the piece bit by bit in small units, I wish to impart wholeness to form and decoration. The form is dependent on the ornamentation and vice versa. Some artists see a conflict between technical performance and a spontaneous creative process. I do not. The source of specific pieces usually is a result of

## Creating Colored-Porcelain Patterns

I started to make ornaments out of colored white stoneware, and I began composing them into different fabric and basket patterns. After a short time, I noticed that I had to add up to 20% of certain stains in order to get the desired color. I realized that this method of coloring was far too expensive, not only for the students, but also for me with an eye toward my future work. I observed that colored porcelain offered me the range of colors I desired and wondered if it was possible to wrap stoneware pieces with thin sheets of colored porcelain. This would be cheaper than coloring white stoneware all the way through. Using slip was out of the question, because I wanted to use the plastic properties and qualities of the clay.

To my great surprise, this technique worked perfectly, despite the 10% shrinkage difference between the porcelain and the stoneware. This combination only worked if the stoneware contained approximately 40% molochite grog. With this success, I was able to continue working with quite large, thick stoneware pieces yet still achieve the bright colors of porcelain.

I begin by packing layers of different shapes and colors together. I follow a sketch to keep track of which color and shape is underneath. When the block is complete, I cut thin sheets at the cross section of the block to produce a thin, usable pattern.

For many years, I have been rolling these thin sheets of patterned colored porcelain on top of slabs of stoneware (any size) or wrapping the sheets around stoneware coils that are up to 1¼ inches thick

**Using small extrusions, coils and slabs of colored porcelain, a pattern is constructed by layering, dissecting and reassembling until it is sufficiently complex.**

a technical experiment. I feel I have reached the point at which the technical aspects have become a familiar, natural and unforced part of my creative process.

Happily, I once noticed a man shaking his head with his nose five centimeters above a piece of mine. He said he was frustrated because he could not get close enough. He felt that the only way to explore the wealth of nuances and details was to actually creep into the surface himself. Although he was frustrated, I was happy, because my goal is to seduce the spectator into a visual voyage of discovery. I want to create an environment in which the viewer can be pushed to experience and explore some of my own fascination with the magical and complex natural world. The closer one gets, and the more time one spends, the more details are waiting to be discovered.

I have reached the limit of this rope technique of mine, so I might have to phone my always helpful and wise colleague Arne Åse for advice. I know he would laugh heartily saying, "Really, Elina, you think you have reached the limit? That is interesting. I can assure you that it all really begins now." And I know he would be right.

# Pitcher Perfect
## Soft-Slab Construction

*by Elizabeth Kendall*

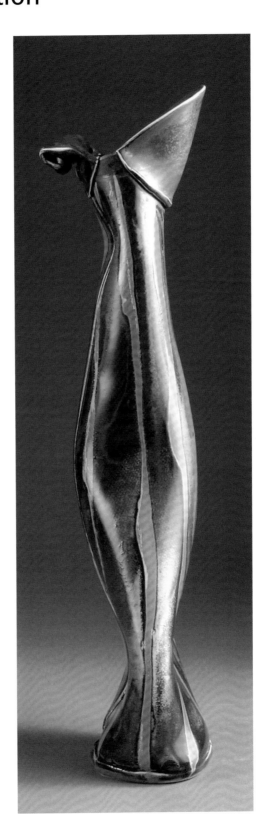

I t's difficult to say which I enjoy more: the handbuilding process or the nature of the porcelain that I use. I love how porcelain behaves, how it flows and bends, and how the process allows me to explore this behavior. There is give and take between my hands and the clay, which both directs the process and contributes to the finished feel of the piece. Even making a simple pitcher allows me to express a feeling and to leave a record of my touch. I handbuild my slab forms from very soft, very thin, right out of the bag porcelain. Because the clay is so thin, I often get a little slumping during firing, which enhances the soft, relaxed look of the finished work. The clay is not wet or sticky while soft, as it would be were it thrown on the wheel. This makes my process very immediate; I don't have to wait for the form to set up before altering. The pitcher that I take out of the kiln always offers some surprise. The give and take that I set in motion has been resolved by the heat of the kiln, the varied thickness of the glaze materials and interactions

**Pitcher, 14 inches in height, porcelain, soft-slab construction, by Elizabeth Kendall.**

between neighboring pieces during the firing. This blend of art and science, of planning and surprise, keeps me going back to the studio for more.

I've found it useful to streamline a few steps in the process, especially at the beginning. Every form starts with a slab, so I usually make slabs from a whole bag of clay in one session. Roll out ¼-inch-thick slabs of clay and trim to create a rectangular section (figure 1). If making several

slabs, stack them with layers of plastic in between. Make sure no air is trapped between layers, and that the plastic is smooth and wrinkle free.

To produce slabs that take advantage of the bends and slumps that occur during the making and firing, use a French rolling pin and roll the slab to about ⅛-inch thick (figure 2). A French rolling pin is made from a single piece of wood, thicker in the middle and tapered toward each end. Because your hands touch the wood that's touching the clay, you'll have a better sense of how easily the clay is moving. You can also place the thicker middle of the pin directly on the part of the clay you want to thin.

After each pass, flip the slab over so it doesn't stick to the canvas, and then turn it 90° so the next pass stretches the clay in a different direction. This repeated rolling also helps to gradually get rid of excess moisture. As the slab gets thinner and flimsier, sandwich it between two pieces of canvas or SlabMat to keep it from tearing or stretching. The SlabMat is a dense paper that will not buckle when wet, and is great for flipping slabs (figure 3) and moving wet work around the studio. Switch surfaces and rolling pins as they get damp.

Cut a trapezoidal shape (figure 4), then cut a slight curve along the bottom edge. Cutting freehand guarantees distinct shapes, with something spontaneous and unexpected at the end. Before cutting, make sure the slab is not stuck to your work surface. A stuck slab will stretch and distort when you try to lift the sides.

To prevent extra thickness at the seam, use a pony roller to bevel and thin the long sides (figure 5). This gives a finished organic edge that keeps with the feeling of the piece.

Place the rolling pin on top of the slab for internal support, and slide your hand and arm under the edge of the slab without distorting or stretching the edge (figure 6). Carefully lift one length up first and onto the top of the rolling pin and then the other.

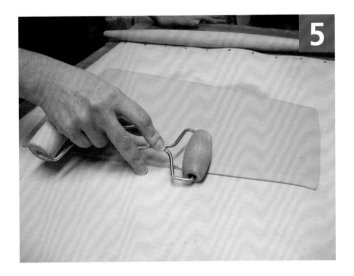

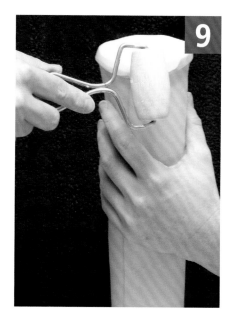

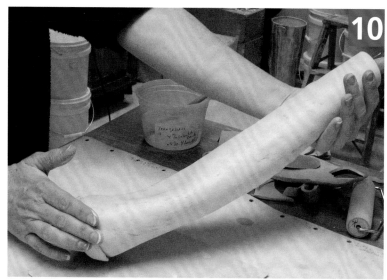

and develop weak spots if it starts to fold (figure 8). Try not to wiggle the material too much and always work with dry hands. Because the slab is so thin, you need to work fairly quickly. Place the cylinder onto a slab and cut out a piece that extends about ¹/₈-inch beyond the edge. Push down gently into the base, then lift and tap the cylinder up and down to compress and attach two pieces.

While upside down, use a roller to compress the bottom onto the cylinder and to roll the edge of the base along the cylinder wall (figure 9). This provides an interesting undulating edge and ensures the strength of the union. Roll the lower corner of the newly joined base along the work surface to further compress and seal the joint, and to soften the seam (figure 10). The whole profile begins to soften as it bends back and forth while rolling.

Gently compress the seam with your hand and finish sealing it using a roller (figure 7). If the slab is fresh and moist, it isn't necessary to score or slip the seams. In fact, it's easy to get the slab too wet. If this happens, the seam will stick or stretch.

Quickly raise the cylinder to a vertical position so it won't flatten

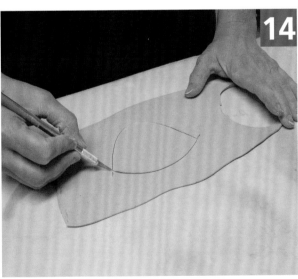

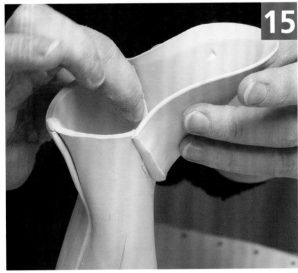

To create an undulating form with sweeping curves, gently squeeze the cylinder with the base of your hands to coax the form out of round (figure 11). Turn the form 45° and move your hand up pushing the sides in at about the point where a waist would be (figure 12). Pushing inward causes parts of the form to bulge more or less revealing a stomach and derriere. Sometimes the bulging needs to be redirected and the waist redefined (figure 13). Use a banding wheel so you can look at the work from all sides and make sure the body reference works.

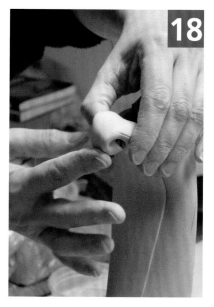

Cut a small U-shape from a very thin slab for the spout (figure 14). Measure and mark the placement on the form, and bevel and thin the pouring edge with the roller. Then roll along the edge of the spout that attaches to the pot. Exaggerate the flat or cut edge to echo the irregular line where the base meets the bottom wall and the exposed seam along the back. Trace the placement of the spout onto the pitcher, and cut an opening ⅛ inch on the inside edge of the tracing. Pinch the cut edge of the spout to thin and soften before attaching, and use gentle pressure to join the spout to the pitcher (figure 15).

A small embellishment where a handle might have started can balance the forward thrust of the spout.

Cut a small triangle of very thin clay and bevel the edges. Bend the two sides of the triangle into the middle making a cone leaving the bottom open (figure 16). Sandwich the top edge of the pitcher rim inside the cone and seal with gentle pressure (figure 17). Roll the cone into a spiral and keep some of the air inside to capture a puffy feeling. Support the sides of the cone with one hand while rolling the tip of the cone in and under (figure 18). The sides may open a bit and cracks may form, so watch carefully. Leave the openings and cracks if they look interesting or smooth them according to taste. Wrap the pitcher loosely with plastic to slow the drying and even out the moisture.

# Marc Leuthold
## An Illusion of Motion

*by Sarah G. Wilkins*

Fluted wheels, disks and conical forms dominate Marc Leuthold's body of work. In each, intricately carved radii emanate from a finely detailed center, creating an illusion of motion, relying on a subtle tension between symmetry and asymmetry. The centrifugal effect is hypnotic. "I hope to project the viewer into a timeless, wordless dimension," Leuthold says.

Working clay in any capacity often requires a serial approach. And in repetition of the same form is the record of subtle refinement, of nuance, of the passage of time from moment to moment. The ceramics artist knows that disciplined repetition is, in fact, an evolutionary tool. Whether it be the vessel or sculptural object, a ceramist may spend years exploring a single form.

Since changes in the carved wheels are subtle, the casual observer might well assume that Leuthold merely repeats himself, cloning duplicates. Nothing could be further from the truth. "Each of the wheels and cones I make is a unique individual," he maintains. "I'd be utterly bored if

the process became too repetitious. I like the subtle changes, the infinite permutations of the form possible in clay. It's a dialogue, or a dance. The maker acts, and the material responds."

Leuthold carves the thick leather-hard disks by hand. Each delicate fissure is carefully wrought; every detail is exacting. The process remains largely intuitive, resulting in a chain of deviations or mutations that defy rational analysis.

"Mutations" is an especially appropriate term here. It is clear that

**"Receptors, Turkish series," to 4½ inches in height, carved porcelain, bisque fired to cone 04.**

Leuthold generates related species, which metamorphose over time, and that he also deliberately fabricates "decayed" works. Some forms are virtually static; some are evolving and some are declining, according to the artist.

Any attempt to uncover further meanings in the work produces a restless oscillation of associations. Viewers may recognize classic forms—the solar disk, the mechanical cog or turbine, radiating forms in nature, waves of wind and water. The circular format is dense with symbolic meaning in every culture, expressive of unity, order and focus. Prayer wheels, medicine wheels, stone circles, the Gothic Rose Window . . . the list of such references is long. Like mandalas, Leuthold's wheels express the mac-

rocosm through the microcosm, and they are indeed mesmerizing.

Spherical models of the universe have always fascinated him. Early in his career he studied the circular diagrams of Jakob Boehme, a 17th-century German mystic. "Boehme used geometry to communicate ideas. Very abstract. Very linear. He used schematic symbols for actors in dramas based on his mystical revelations—precisely located at points within a circle."

Bohme's elegant diagrams and Leuthold's wheels suggest the existence of a "sacred geometry," of a world both rational and mysterious. Such lofty associations are slippery at best, though. Leuthold's brand of reductive abstraction allows for multiple shifts and takes—but firmly denies conclusions. "I prefer abstraction that is multi-referential, that can't be easily explained," he says.

The viewer may simply choose to let the work operate directly on the senses. Leuthold cites his interest in the purely decorative encrusted medieval ornament, made only to adorn and enhance. He is especially fond of the gold and garnet brooches of the Merovingian period. These pieces were made of roughly shaped cells of gold, each embracing a brilliant red garnet. "They look crude if you inspect them closely, but the total effect is rich and engaging. The repetition and abundance somehow make them beautiful. My work consists of cells and flutes that operate the same way. In making my cuts with the knife, I allow imperfections to remain untouched. I believe this adds energy and vitality to the work."

Viewers do respond viscerally to these forms. The differing surfaces are highly tactile, and the subtle colors further define character. Leuthold says he uses matt glazes sometimes, but he also likes the velvety surface of white underfired clay. Lately he has been using pigmented porcelain, with a hint of color. The colorant is mixed throughout the clay body, and the sculpture left unglazed. "I add Mason stains to a white porcelain slip. I don't measure....I just add colorant by eye. A lot of stain makes a darker color. I sieve the mixture and dry it on plaster, and then add this colored paste to the clay body. It creates a different texture, a chalky surface."

Leuthold carving a 65-inch-diameter stoneware wheel to be cast in bronze.

The effect is slightly artificial, ambiguous. Often the viewer is not quite sure what material the wheels are actually made of. This is intentional.

The central cavity of the wheels has become more elaborate in recent years. Leuthold calls them simply "portholes." The viewer is free to make more imaginative associations. It can be read as a symbol of

**To carve the center of the disk, Leuthold balanced himself on a platform just a few inches above the working surface.**

calm or sanctuary, an "eye of the storm," especially when the radii are more fluid and wavelike. Sometimes the implied forces seem to be rotating inward, contracting into a vortex or whirlpool. Other wheels appear to be expanding outward—radiating, like the sun.

On a corporeal level, the wheel as a whole suggests an iris with the center as pupil. The empty center may be understood as "blind" and void, like a camera shutter; or latent, as in the concept of the "third eye," the symbol for intuitive wisdom. The omnipotent and all-seeing Divine Eye is yet another interpretation. When seen together in an exhibition, the opening and closing of the portholes is subtly felt, the winking animation of the disembodied eye.

Although a strong sense of primal unity characterizes his work, there is a hint that situations of duality

are emerging. At times in the past he has displayed two wheels side-by-side on their metal stands in twin or sibling relationship. But lately these familial forms have become less alike, with greater contrasts between them. These "odd couples" invite the viewer to question their symbiosis, to understand their apparent magnetism.

Expanding the dyad concept, Leuthold began to make 4- to 6-inch-diameter cone shapes and to display them alongside the larger wheels, which range from 12 inches to 28 inches in diameter. The large orb and its smaller satellite are placed together, frontally in a single plane, arranged as though they are mere specimens.

The small cones range in shape from shallow and open dishes to obvious trumpets with definite tunnels, and may have flutes on the in-

**Working on a large scale allowed Leuthold to vary the carving depth more than had been possible with smaller work.**

ner surfaces. Presented horizontally, the trumpets invite inspection of their interiors. Displayed adjacent to a wheel, the small cones inspire myriad associations—horn, funnel, comet— even "satellite dish" comes to mind, in the case of the shallower forms. Leuthold refers to all members of the series generically as "Receptors."

During a symposium in the Izmir region of Turkey, he was inspired to create a series of completely smooth, small cones, carving and hollowing the bone-dry porcelain, a method used by early 20th-century ceramist Adelaide Robineau. The smooth cones clearly relate to the pure biomorphic forms of such artists as Louise Bourgeois and Jean Arp. Leuthold calls these smooth cones suggestively "ears," as if they were sensory organs, held within the powerful field of the companion wheel.

"The ear forms evolved from the cones, which in turn evolved from the wheels, so it seems natural to group them together," comments Leuthold. "Like a zoologist looking at distantly related mammals, I find groups of similar objects intriguing. They speak to each other. They have a synergism."

But if the cones and ears grew out of the wheels, they do appear to be distinctly different genera—notably, these fledgling life forms are born "ancient" and decayed. In striking contrast to the perfection and unity implied by the wheels, the small cones and ears, with their irregular features, are presented in an obviously fragmented state. This is not unprecedented. Leuthold sometimes intentionally breaks a large wheel after the firing, selecting a particular piece, a "shard," which he continues to subtract from until the fragment becomes a fan-shaped form; at that point, he may further modify the surface before mounting the piece. Most ceramics artists keep shard collections on studio shelves for future reference and inspiration. But it is a different thing to deliberately create such a shard and display it as a finished work. In Leuthold's view, the wheel shards do not merely attest to the fragility of the ceramic process, but serve as monuments to the highly romantic notion of "permanent imperfection."

The more recent small cones and ears are likewise intended to suggest the maker's attempts at reclamation, although they are purposely altered and broken at the leather-hard stage, rather than after firing. In this artificial aging process is implied a sense of fleeting time, the decomposition of earthly things, and even the wistfulness of the human concern to collect and display such artifacts. So if the symmetrical wheels refer to a state of idealized perfection, the small conical forms clearly suggest transition and impermanence. With their dyadic placement next to the regal and more captivating wheels, the ear and cone "Receptors" seem an earthly bridge to that more rarefied realm.

While he continues to make his 12- to 28-inch ceramic wheel forms, Leuthold has just finished his largest sculpture ever—a bronze wheel commissioned for an outdoor sculpture garden, measuring over 5 feet in diameter and 8 inches in depth. Eighteen months in progress, the work was completed by the Tallix Foundry, just north of New York City.

Leuthold had planned to carve the clay originals for the bronze directly—with the same large kitchen knife he always uses when carving his porcelain and stoneware wheels. But he was not at all sure he could capture the spirit of the smaller wheels in a scale four times his usual size. It was a leap of faith. "I was anxious at first." But soon, he says, he found it "exhilarating" to carve on such a scale.

Each side of the wheel was carved separately. Over 1200 pounds of white stoneware clay was divided into two 5-foot-wide clay disks. For much of the work, Leuthold had to lie on a rig hovering over the leather-hard clay, pulling the knife with both hands. The radii took a full six days to carve, roughly three days for each disk. He had a limited window for carving, as foundry technicians were scheduled to pour the rubber and wax molds for the subsequent stages of the lost-wax process. So there was no time to stop and contemplate—just a sense of diving in and going on instinct, trusting to intuition.

"In preparation for this sculpture, I began to think of carving in a way that capitalizes on the thickness of the clay, carving the flutes so they vary in height within the clay mass. Where the flutes really dive down deep, I began to think of these as cupped areas or depressions instead of a series of linear fissures."

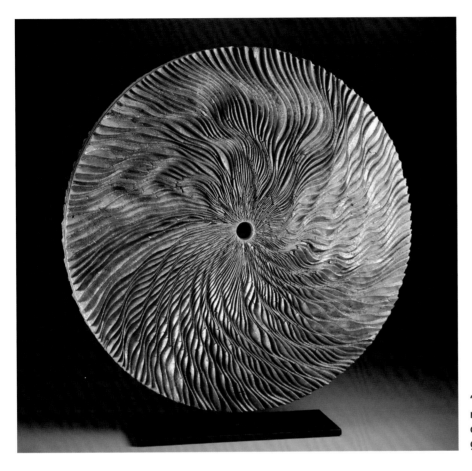

**"Red Wheel, Bohme Series,"** 17 inches in diameter, carved earthenware, with glaze, fired to cone 010.

These undulating fissures presented a challenge to the foundry technicians, who find it difficult to cast deep undercuts in any sculpture. And the carved stoneware wheel had more than 200. "I was skeptical that the fluid quality of the clay original would actually translate to the bronze," Leuthold admits, "but the Tallix technicians were so positive, they gave me confidence. In fact, Bruce Ostwald should be credited as a collaborator on this project, he helped so much."

At one point in carving the second side, Leuthold's venerable knife broke—the only knife he had used in 15 years of carving clay. With no time to spare, in an unintentional nod to his Swiss heritage, he finished the second disk with a Swiss army knife. Both clay disks were then subjected to the mold process before the molten bronze was poured. After cooling, the bronze was "chased," or burnished by hand (which took several weeks), then completed with a turquoise patina. The single opening—the eye cavity—was gold-plated.

After carving the large disks for the bronze, Leuthold says he is considering expanding the scale of his claywork. "Of course it is technically possible to create such large works

"Diptych," 20 inches in width, carved porcelain, bisque fired to cone 04, by Marc Leuthold, Potsdam, New York.

entirely in ceramics….I can imagine making clay wheels as large, or even larger than the bronze."

Yet even as he widens his scope and scale, Leuthold continues to pursue new ideas in his more intimate wheels and cones. "I like the intensity of focus required in the microcosm. I can draw the viewer's attention to details and nuances generally overlooked in a larger work," he explains. "Also, in making the bronze, I missed the unique physical effects of the firing process—how the clay sags and moves, even how it cracks. Each piece goes through an individual metamorphosis."

Such statements abound in the world of ceramics, where artists struggle in their attempts to harness this often unruly medium. The key to success would seem to be an attitude of flexibility and persistence. Leuthold compares working in clay to "sculpting" his garden, another of his passions. "You can assert your dominance working with a static material—building a house, for example. But you can't have it all your way in the garden," he says. "Your vulnerable creation can be wantonly destroyed by storms, freezes, insects, diseases. Anyone who has worked consistently with plants learns great patience. The same is true with clay."

# Jennifer Lee
## The Circumnavigation of Form

*by David Whiting*

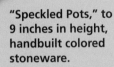

"Speckled Pots," to
9 inches in height,
handbuilt colored
stoneware.

Jennifer Lee is a potter of si-
lence. She does not issue artist's statements and, although
naturally interested in ceramics de-
bates, she does not actively engage in
them. She prefers simply to focus on
her work, to make pots that evolve
slowly in the small studio at the rear
of her house in London. They are objects of exacting clarity, vessels that
do not appear to have changed that
radically over the years—until you
compare what she makes today to
those she made in the mid 1980s.
Then, one sees the subtle and grad-
ual developments. While her palette
has deepened and broadened, there
is also an increased discipline and
precision. Hers is an art that is built
up and then honed down. Like stones
on the beach that have matured geo-
logically and then been smoothed
by the elements, her pots appear to
encompass a great deal about our
world in concentrated form. They
have no "message" as such. You will
find no politics or polemicism here.
What her work does express is the
continuing renewal of what the late
Joanna Constantinidis called "la-

tent energy," of a tension built up in
the rising clay through the fingers,
a kind of upward movement made
through the symmetry and asymmetry of form and the stratified layers
within. Yet, while these objects are
suggestive of many things, they are
also quietly and confidently self-con-
tained.

Jennifer Lee's creative certainty
brought her success at a young age.
Since leaving London's Royal College of Art, she has gone on to ex-
hibit all around the world and is
represented now in over 25 public
collections. She has also had two
museum retrospectives. Though
long established in Camberwell, just
south of the River Thames, her roots
are very different. She was born into
a farming family in Aberdeenshire,
Scotland, a landscape to which she
often returns. In the mid 1970s, after
a brief flirtation with physiotherapy,
she went to Edinburgh College of

**"Pale Pot," 11 inches in height, handbuilt stoneware, with colored stoneware vein and rim.**

**"Dark Pot, Tilted Rim," 11 inches in height, handbuilt colored stoneware.**

Art to study ceramics and tapestry. She then spent several months on a traveling scholarship in the United States, where she researched Southwest Indian prehistoric ceramics and visited West Coast potters, including Peter Voulkos, Paul Soldner and Ken Price. Upon returning to

Britain, she completed her ceramics studies at the Royal College of Art.

What is striking about the work is its constancy, the way in which she has been able to explore and fathom the constitution of clay and delineation of form through the endless possibilities of the cylinder and the bowl. Within these self-imposed parameters, her journey has, in a sense, moved inward, gauging and regauging the interaction of profile and surface, interior and exterior, volume and lift. Right from the beginning, there was a concern with poise and balance; the curvature of her pots swelling from a narrow base that creates a minimal point of contact with the surface on which they rest. It appears to make them float. But more than this, her pots often present, as Oliver Watson once observed, "an asymmetric disjuncture which disturbs their classical profiles."

This is found not only in the sedimentary motion of the work, but in Lee's approach to contour. Rims often lean or deviate in other ways. She has made "shelf rims," which partially close the opening and naturally transform the nature and light of the contained space. Lips have been tilted and extended outward. Some pieces have had softly emerging ridges—interventions that grow seamlessly from the main body. They clearly relate to some of the most elemental examples of early pots, from Bronze Age bowls to Ancient Egyptian wares found on numerous grave sites. Yet she also achieves a precision that distills and condenses what she has seen and experienced. They are pots that, singly or in related sculptural groups, have a very modern intelligence.

The superb vessels made in predynastic Egypt, on the Upper Nile, certainly have affiliations with Lee's work. These early pots, made from red Nile silt or hard, buff marl clay, are among the most abstract we know. The egyptologist Jaromír Málek said that they are remarkable for their "subdued elegance," surely a description we could apply to Lee's ceramics. She too builds up her shapes from coils or strips of rolled clay, but whereas the black crests that characterize those Egyptian pots were achieved through

"Sand-Grained Pot, Smoky Spiral," 8 inches in height, handbuilt colored stoneware.

the firing process, Lee's color is introduced into the clay by mixing in metallic oxides. These carefully judged tonal variations create a symbiosis between inside and outside that avoids the dividing skin of a covering glaze. Moreover, the horizontal and diagonal layers and veins of staining add to the sensation that these objects hover and shift in space. They have a posture and equilibrium that is far from static. Those Egyptian pots were burnished to create their glossy surfaces. Lee's patient abrading and burnishing completes that sense of wind-polished geology, but to see them solely as evocations or excavations of landscape is rather limiting. One critic has recently related her art to color-field painting and her best work has a comparable geometry of hues. Reminiscent of Mark Rothko, there is a similar ambiguity of depth and space. While some pots are more arid, with coarser speckled stains, others have a more liquid and vaporous quality, like watercolor or a bank of rain cloud. In fact, Lee is just as much a painter as she is a potter, but whose abstraction is expressed in the three-dimensional terms of enclosed form.

Looking back at the work Lee produced in the early 1980s, after she left the Royal College, we realize what a different kind of potter she was in the milieu of that time. Her work did not exemplify the loud color, glitz and baroque forms of so many of that generation. Instead, her pots seemed, as they remain,

disarmingly simple. They continue to allude to natural and manmade archetypes, to history and the passage of time. Their broad frame of reference removes them from any sense of the specific. Today, the pots seem more economic in form, but increasingly complex and virtuosic in their distribution and densities of color. Some pieces are best appreciated when placed with near relations, to fully understand how a formal idea is developed and carried through before she moves on. Lee's art is not concerned with fashion or sudden stylistic changes of gear. It evolves on its own terms, regardless of the temperature in the outside world.

"Olive Pot, Dark Olive Pot, Dark Pot," to 10 inches in height, handbuilt colored stoneware, by Jennifer Lee, London, England.

# Jan Schachter
## Melding Form and Function

*by Linda Mau*

Jan Schachter is committed to making functional ware; pots to be used, made with care and made with strong design. Though Schachter believes functional ware is sometimes overlooked by jurors, her passion for melding form and function has not gone unnoticed.

Although Schachter discovered the joy of clay when she was only six years old, she did not become a potter until after graduating in microbiology from the University of Massachusetts. Like many artists, she realized that she was not suited to life in an office. She then returned to clay, attending classes at Greenwich House Pottery in New York City. After a move to Westchester County, New York, she worked and studied at the Clay Art Center in Port Chester and the Old Church Cultural Center (now the Art School at Old Church) in Demarest, New Jersey. It wasn't until after she and her family moved to California that she became a full-time, award-winning, functional potter.

Her studio is located in the hills west of Stanford University. It is as

well designed and functional as her pottery. It sits among ancient oak trees and was constructed to blend with the Spanish architecture of her home. She had the rare opportunity of designing her studio space, including considerations for efficient cleaning and ware handling. Her kilns, an Olsen 24 and an electric Crucible kiln for bisque, are housed in a covered outdoor area. The clay studio includes a standing Brent wheel. Like many production potters, she finds that raising her wheel to allow her to stand while throwing has greatly decreased back problems. There is also a trimming wheel, slab roller,

"Storage Jar," 8½ inches in height, thrown custom stoneware, with oak wood ash glaze, fired to cone 10 in reduction. One of Schachter's signature design elements is an extruded coil handle wrapped with unglazed Black Mountain Clay.

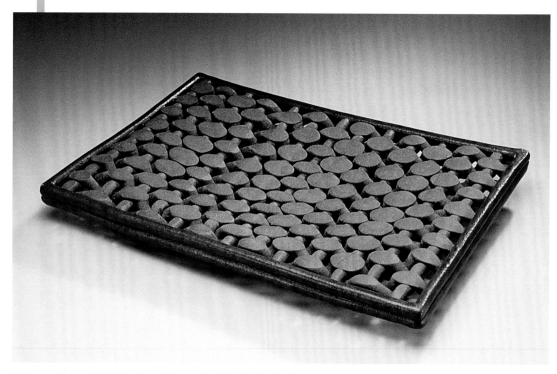

"Woven Plate," 15¼ inches in length, slab-built Black Mountain Clay, unglazed except the edge, which is glazed with Black Oak Wood Ash Glaze, fired to cone 10 in reduction.

extruder and worktables. She sorts her work by form, glaze or clay body on the open shelves lining the room. Pieces made for customers requesting specific sizes and glazes are kept separate to ensure consistency, and to make shipping and invoicing more efficient.

Schachter works on clay, either in her studio or in related ceramic activities, every day. With this amount of production, she markets her work in various ways. She hosts an open studio at her home twice a year with a small group of other invited artists. She also participates in the two very successful festivals put on by the Association of Clay & Glass Artists of California (ACGA). She does

a limited number of commissions, supplies various galleries across the country, and also sells her work through Guild.com and her personal website www.janschachter.com.

Schachter's style has evolved over the years, yet remains recognizable. Although best known for her covered containers with unique coil handles, she constantly explores new designs and forms. "Although I frequently make utilitarian stoneware, I occasionally blend my clay, textile and basketry experiences by weaving 'plates' out of clay," she says. Woven plates take a great deal of concentration and time as the limitations of the clay create special challenges for the artist.

## Stamped Slab Plates

*by Jan Schachter*

Some of the most satisfying pieces to make in my repertoire are slab plates. Getting away from the wheel allows me to experiment with new shapes and surface decoration.

Starting with wedged clay, I roll -inch slabs using a slab roller. I use old, soft pillowcases cut in half to facilitate turning the clay onto a canvas-covered board. A few rolls in both directions with a rolling pin seems to reduce warping. The clay is then cut using a metal square as a guide. Sometimes I tear the edges against the square and sometimes I retain a raw edge. The edges are smoothed with a damp sponge and I stamp my mark on the bottom. Using another cloth and board, the clay is flipped to the surface that will become the top.

Again using the square, I lightly designate where the finger marks will go, defining the portion of the plate I will "mark." I have a large box of stamps I have accumulated over the years. My favorite is a wooden roller from India used for massage. Its teeth leave rows of inverted pyramids.

To shape the plate, I raise the sides by holding on to the cloth, and slide lengths of 2×6-inch board underneath that have been cut in half lengthwise on a 45° angle. I have props cut to many lengths so I can make plates in any proportion. Then I run my fingers along the premarked finger lines to press the bottom flat. I adjust the props to leave the plate as true as possible while it sets up. When the boards are removed, feet can be added and the shape can be corrected.

After bisque firing, I brush on Black Oak Wood Ash Glaze to fill the teeth marks. Excess is scraped off until the glaze is only in the pyramids. The plate is then dipped either in Laura's Turquoise or my Cream Oak Ash glaze.

**"Slab Plate," 14 inches in length, slab-built custom stoneware, with Laura's Turquoise over Black Oak Wood Ash Glaze in the roller marks, fired to cone 10 in reduction.**

**Casserole, 8½ inches in diameter, thrown custom stoneware, with Black Oak Wood Ash Glaze, fired to cone 10 in reduction, with extruded coil handle wrapped with unglazed clay, by Jan Schachter, Portola Valley, California.**

To maintain consistency throughout her line of work, Schachter limits the number of glazes she uses. Since each piece is monochromatic, the glaze must be rich and varied enough to provide visual interest. After much testing, she modified both a black and cream-colored ash glaze to make them stable and appropriate for utilitarian ware. For variety and contrast, she uses a rich green glaze, Laura's Turquoise, attributed to Steven Hill. But the application is her own—she mixes it thick and applies it to bisqueware, not greenware as Hill does—producing subtle variations in the color.

## Recipes

### Black Oak Wood Ash Glaze
Cone 10 Reduction

| | |
|---|---|
| Washed Oak Wood Ash . . . . . . . . | 49 % |
| Kona F-4 Feldspar . . . . . . . . . . . | 24 |
| Tennessee Ball Clay . . . . . . . . . . | 27 |
| | 100 % |
| Add: Bentonite . . . . . . . . . . . . . | 20% |
| Copper Carbonate. . . . . . . . | 10% |
| Manganese Dioxide . . . . . . . | 10% |

### Laura's Turquoise
Cone 10 Reduction

| | |
|---|---|
| Whiting. . . . . . . . . . . . . . . . . . . | 37.4% |
| Custer Feldspar . . . . . . . . . . . . . | 23.3 |
| EPK Kaolin. . . . . . . . . . . . . . . . . | 30.0 |
| Silica . . . . . . . . . . . . . . . . . . . . . | 9.3 |
| | 100.0% |
| Add: Bentonite . . . . . . . . . . . . . | 1.9% |
| Cobalt Carbonate . . . . . . . . | 0.2% |
| Copper Carbonate. . . . . . . . | 3.0% |
| Powdered Rutile . . . . . . . . . | 2.8% |

### Cream Oak Ash Glaze
Cone 10 Reduction

| | |
|---|---|
| Washed Wood Ash. . . . . . . . . . . | 50 % |
| Kona F-4 Feldspar . . . . . . . . . . . | 30 |
| Tennessee Ball Clay . . . . . . . . . . | 20 |
| | 100 % |
| Add: Bentonite . . . . . . . . . . . . . | 2 % |
| Zircopax . . . . . . . . . . . . . . . | 20% |

The ashes are screened to remove any wood or charcoal, etc. They are then mixed with water and allowed to settle. The water is decanted and new water added and mixed in. This process is repeated 3 or 4 times until the water no longer feels soapy. The wet ashes are scooped into a large basin lined with a cloth to help wick away the water, and left to dry.